# Hardship
## and Hope

# Hardship and Hope

## AMERICA AND THE
## GREAT DEPRESSION

### VICTORIA SHERROW

Twenty-First Century Books

Brookfield, Connecticut

Twenty-First Century Books
A Division of The Millbrook Press
2 Old New Milford Road
Brookfield, CT 06804

**Library of Congress Cataloging-in-Publication Data**
Sherrow, Victoria.
Hardship and hope : America and the Great Depression /
by Victoria Sherrow.
p.    cm.
Includes bibliographical references and index.
Summary: Examines the causes and conditions of the difficult
economic times known as the Great Depression.
1. Depressions—1929—United States—Juvenile literature.
[1. Depressions—1929. 2. United States—Economic
conditions—1918–1945.] I. Title.
HB3717 1929.S54                                    96-28970
338.5'42—dc20                                           CIP
                                                         AC

ISBN 0-8050-4178-8

*Designed by Kelly Soong*

Printed in the United States of America

3   5   7   9   10   8   6   4   2

*To my mother, Lillian, with love*

# Contents

# 1

## *Thin Ice*

We don't have to worry about anything. No nation in the history of the world was ever sitting as pretty. If we want anything, all we have to do is go and buy it on credit. So that leaves us without any economic problem whatever, except perhaps some day to have to pay for them. But we are certainly not thinking about that this early.[1]

—WILL ROGERS, SEPTEMBER 1929

When these ironic words appeared in the newspaper column written by the popular humorist Will Rogers, the United States was nearing the end of a prosperous decade. During the 1920s, the overall mood in the nation had been upbeat. President Herbert Hoover had even declared, "We in America today are nearer to the final triumph over poverty than ever before in the history of any land."[2]

People saw signs of prosperity: Many workers were earning higher wages than ever before. Factories were using new machinery and electricity to produce more goods. Automobiles, cigarettes, radios, and other items from America were being sold around the world. Americans enjoyed more material comforts as they bought cars and new home appliances, often "on credit," making a down payment and agreeing to pay the rest in installments. Some had even ventured into the stock market for the first time.

Yet, about a month after Rogers wrote those words, the nation had entered into the deepest and most prolonged economic depression in its history. The Great Depression stretched from October of 1929 into 1941, reaching its depths in 1932. During those years, millions of Americans slid into poverty as they lost their jobs, homes, savings, and possessions. The poor became poorer, struggling to survive. Thousands of people, including children, died from starvation or from the lack of health care. Many young people gave up their dreams of careers, education, or marriage. Thousands of homeless people wandered around the country.

What had caused such a calamity? Historians have debated the causes of the Great Depression ever since it took place. The Depression officially began on the day of the stock market "Crash"—October 29, 1929. But trouble had been brewing for years. A number of events, business practices, and economic conditions during the 1920s set the stage for disaster.

## FROM FARMS TO FACTORIES

Until the mid-1800s, most Americans were farmers. Families usually grew, raised, made, or bartered for whatever they needed. The arrival of the Industrial Revolution and a money-based economy changed the way most people made a living. Many took jobs in factories, businesses, or transportation-related industries, receiving wages for their labor.

Some, often newly arrived immigrants, took difficult jobs in coal mines, steel mills, textile mills, and garment factories. They built roads, canals, bridges, and railway systems. The workday was long, the wages low. For example, a garment worker in 1910 might receive only six dollars for a seventy-hour week.

World War I (1914–18) boosted the general economy. The nation supplied airplanes, tanks, weapons, ammunition, and raw materials—steel, oil, rubber, and coal—to the Allies. Farmers stepped up production as America exported food to the stricken nations. The United States finally entered the war in 1917 after Germany sank some American ships and threatened to blockade the British Isles.

After the war, businesses and factories continued to produce goods, now geared for consumers rather than military use. By the 1920s, many jobs revolved around the automobile industry. In 1919, there were 7 million passenger cars in the United States, a figure that grew by about a million each year during the twenties. Auto making provided more than 4 million jobs, in addition to many jobs in related industries—steel, oil, glass, rubber, paint, and road building. A few auto companies controlled almost all production, as was true in other industries. Ford, General Motors, and Chrysler made 90 percent of all American cars and trucks.

Factory output rose with the coming of electrical power and efficient new machines. The radio and home appliance industries boomed. So did the sales of luxury items, since the wealthiest Americans had so much purchasing power.

An increased demand for housing and for places of business yielded more jobs in the building trades. School enrollments rose, too, so new schools were needed. Higher family incomes meant that more young people could finish high school and even go to college rather than take jobs in their early teens.

Shorter workweeks and new electric appliances gave some Americans more leisure time. Recreation increased, as people went golfing, bowling, and roller-skating, played tennis, or visited amusement parks. "Talking pictures" arrived during the late 1920s. Comedies, adventure films, romances, westerns, and epics based on biblical stories were shown in entertainment parks and theaters, along with newsreels capturing events around the world.

The economy tends to be strong when people have faith in the future. Feeling confident, and with their leaders promising an even brighter future, Americans of the 1920s bought things before they had saved up enough money to pay for them. They were eager to own automobiles, as well as radios and the home appliances that became available after electricity arrived in communities across America. They were encouraged by ads that hailed wondrous laborsaving devices and the glories of owning one's own car.

By 1929, Americans had accumulated more than $3 billion in outstanding credit debt. Four of every five cars had been bought on credit. Most homes and other real estate were also bought with the help of bank loans, called mortgages. A joke that later circulated during the Depression said that making the first payment for an item bought on credit made a person feel rich; having to make the rest showed him he was not.

Historians have said that credit buying signaled a change in the mood and values of the nation during the twenties. Many Americans abandoned traditional values of thrift and hard work and instead looked for "easy money" and instant gratification.

## THE FREE MARKET

The economic system that evolved in the United States has often been called *laissez-faire*, from French words meaning "let do" (that is, "let people do what they wish"). Under this free-market system of capitalism, people could pursue profit-making enterprises without much interference. No laws dictated what kinds or quantities of goods should be produced. Businesses were not subject to federal regulations or taxes as they are today; nor were there strong unions to protect workers.

Business owners could keep wages low. By 1929, the output of the average American worker was up by more than 40 percent, yet wages increased by a mere 7 percent.[3] Nor did manufacturers lower prices charged to consumers. About 60 percent of all Americans made less than $2,000 a year. Child laborers often worked for pennies an hour under dreadful conditions, a situation regarded as an outrage by reformers. Low wages meant that while there were more goods in the marketplace, most Americans could not afford them.

Through the years, workers had formed labor unions and tried to bargain for better wages and working conditions, sometimes by going "on strike" until demands were met. Strikes were put down by state militias, local police, and strikebreakers hired by the company where the strike was taking place. As a condition of employment, many employers forced workers to sign pledges stating that they would not join a union.

When the labor movement gained momentum during the early 1900s, many business owners labeled it communist-inspired. Most Americans feared the nondemocratic form of government they called "godless communism." Socialist and communist governments had come to power in certain countries, so immigrants from those places, who included Russians and people from southern and eastern Europe, were often viewed with suspicion. In this way, business owners prevented laborers from gaining political power.

## LIMITED PROSPERITY

Since income taxes had just been introduced and were quite low throughout the 1920s, the captains of industry (or "robber barons," as some called them) amassed vast fortunes—millions, even billions, of dollars. Some of the newly rich became famous for their lavish homes, possessions, and lifestyles. Photos of the

"Roaring Twenties" often show carefree fun, typified by "flappers" dancing the Charleston in short skirts, and parties where people drank bootleg gin from bathtubs. Organized criminal networks grew wealthy by selling alcohol in defiance of the Eighteenth Amendment, passed in 1919. The amendment banned making, selling, or buying liquor but it was ignored by people of all socioeconomic levels during what became known as Prohibition.

While millionaires grew richer and made the news, many Americans barely scraped by. Farmers, southern sharecroppers, and African Americans and other minorities were among those for whom "good times" had not arrived. There was severe poverty in Appalachia, a mining area that included parts of Pennsylvania, Kentucky, Tennessee, and West Virginia. The coal industry sagged in competition with petroleum. As orders declined, mine owners dismissed many workers.

Textile companies, mostly in southern states, also saw falling orders and lower profits, followed by worker layoffs. Construction declined during 1928–29, too. By the summer of 1929, the steel industry was operating at 67 percent capacity. Sales of luxury goods—jewelry, expensive cars, and furs—had dropped.

Farmers, who had been producing larger crops during World War I, now had surpluses and often could not make a profit. With little purchasing power, farmers could not buy the goods that American factories were producing in huge numbers.

Extending electric power to rural areas was not profitable, so life on the farm could mean long hours of labor without modern conveniences. When farmers sought government help during the Coolidge administration (1924–29), the president remarked, "Farmers have never made money. I don't believe we can do much about it."[4]

Nor was the "average American" prosperous: About 78 percent of all families had annual incomes less than $3,000, with 40 percent living on less than $1,500, the minimum needed to raise a family adequately at that time. Only 2.3 percent earned more than $10,000 a year. On the eve of the Crash, the 60,000 wealthiest Americans had savings that totaled what was owned by the 25 million poorest. The 24,000 families with the highest incomes in 1929 earned as much as the total earned by the *11 million* with incomes below $1,500.

This uneven distribution of wealth alarmed some people, including future President Herbert Hoover. He wrote, "The economic system cannot survive unless there are real restraints upon unbridled greed or dishonest reach for power."[5]

## A Shaky Economy

Some analysts concluded that the economic "boom" of the twenties rested on a shaky foundation, including a flawed U.S. banking system. Just 1 percent of all financial institutions controlled 46 percent of all banking business in the United States. Herbert Hoover was among the critics, calling banking "the weakest link in our whole economic system."[6]

Relatively few Americans had much control over business. Powerful holding companies owned the stock of several corporations and could decide how to run them all. Author Robert Goldston points out, "Corporate structures became exceedingly intricate . . . Thus, if anything went wrong, fewer and fewer people would be able to predict where the chips might fall, or whose chips they might be."[7]

During World War I, a number of European nations had become indebted to the United States after buying millions of dollars of war materials. After the war, the United States went from being the world's greatest debtor nation to its largest creditor. A debtor nation can export a greater value of goods than it imports, using the difference to help pay off its debts. But, as economist John Kenneth Galbraith points out, "a creditor must import a greater value than it exports if those who owe it money are to have the wherewithal to pay interest and principal."[8] With these imported products coming in, the United States was left with even more goods that Americans could not afford to buy.

## WIDESPREAD SPECULATION

For years, both new and established companies had raised money for growth and development by offering other people the chance to buy shares of their stock. At first, only wealthy Americans bought stocks. As investors, they would often hold stock for years, collecting dividends—percentages of their profits—that many companies paid out on a regular basis. Companies that did well often increased their dividends. At some point, after a stock rose in value, investors or their heirs might sell it at a profit.

During the twenties, more Americans, including people of limited means, bought stocks. The number of stockbrokers rose from 30,000 in 1920 to 71,000 in 1929. Stories spread of people who had made fortunes in the rising stock market, and more Americans saw stocks as a way to quick riches. Many relied on "hot tips" or rumors when buying stocks. Some bought whatever was offered—after all, everything seemed to go up. Those who got lucky warned others they were fools not to take advantage of the booming stock market.

Instead of holding stocks, which is called investing, many sold them for quick profits, a practice called trading. There was widespread speculation as new stocks were issued and people clamored to buy them, regardless of the company's inherent worth. For example, the stock of one new gold-mining company soared in price although the company had only a lease on some unproven land and no earnings yet.

Speculators could buy larger amounts of stock by borrowing part of the money, called buying "on margin." These buyers expected to pay off their loans after selling their stocks at a higher price. Brokerage firms borrowed money from banks to finance such purchases. From 1923 to 1929, loans to brokers rose from $1.5 billion to $6 billion. Corporations and individuals also lent money to brokers, at interest rates as high as 20 percent.[9] So, although the stock market had a high value on paper, far less cash actually backed it up since much of the cost of stocks was borrowed.

Many companies did not use investors' money to build up the business or improve plants and facilities. In some cases, they used this money for their own speculations in the stock market. Large investment trusts—business entities set up for the purpose of issuing and selling stock—also sprang up to take advantage of the boom in investing, further feeding the speculative frenzy.

At the time, there were few federal regulations to control activities on Wall Street, the seat of the New York Stock Exchange, located in New York City. In February 1927, troubled by increasing speculation, the Federal Reserve Board raised the rates that it charged banks on borrowed money. It raised interest rates slightly again in May, but the amount of speculation remained high.

Many people who viewed the stock market as "gambling" continued to place their money in banks, where they received a fixed, guaranteed rate of interest. Yet many banks were also heavily invested in stocks or had lent large sums to brokers. These banks were taking risks with depositors' funds and were not a safe place to keep money.

Investors dabbled in land speculation, as well. Americans were told that the sunny states of Florida and California were good places to buy property. Prospective buyers were told that this land could be resold at large profits as more people settled in these states. But the Florida "land bubble," as it was called, burst in 1926, when people had to sell at a loss. It was a harbinger of things to come.

## TROUBLE ABROAD

After World War I, the United States followed a policy called isolationism—concentrating on domestic affairs and avoiding international matters. Despite President Woodrow Wilson's ardent pleas, Congress had rejected joining the League of Nations, which was organized to improve international relations and provide a forum for resolving differences without violence. Without U.S. support, the League dwindled.

During the postwar years, unstable governments and poor economic conditions plagued Europe. By the 1920s, totalitarian governments controlled Russia and Japan. As Germany's Adolf Hitler and Italy's Benito Mussolini rose to power during the 1930s, many Americans regarded these men as shrill extremists, not likely to rule for long. But the fascist agenda and weakening economy of Europe were to have profound effects on the rest of the world, prolonging the Depression and leading to war.


## A NEW PRESIDENT

During the presidential election of 1924, Calvin Coolidge liked to say, "The business of America is business."[10] This philosophy was echoed by other Republicans, members of the party in power from 1920 to 1932.

In 1928, a new Republican president was elected: Herbert Clark Hoover. A self-made man, Hoover had been orphaned at age eight and reared by an uncle in Oregon. He had worked hard to get through college and become an engineer, eventually running his own firm.

After amassing a personal fortune of several million dollars, Hoover dedicated himself to public service. He headed a committee that brought home Americans who found themselves stranded in Europe after war was declared. When America

Born in Oklahoma on November 4, 1879, William Penn Adair Rogers was descended from Cherokee Indians on both sides of his family and had Irish, Welsh, and English and either German or Dutch ancestors, as well. Growing up, he spent a lot of time outdoors doing ranch chores. Rogers became an expert roper, a talent he perfected later on when he was hired to perform in circuses and Wild West shows, where he was sometimes billed as the "Cherokee Kid."

Rogers later toured America and Europe as a vaudeville star, incorporating rope tricks, jokes, and gags into his act. An avid newspaper reader and observer of people and the political scene, he added commentary on current events to his act. He became a popular star on Broadway and in motion pictures.

From December 1922 until his death in 1935, Rogers wrote for newspapers and magazines: 667 weekly articles, as well as 511 columns and nearly 3,000 short pieces called "The Daily Telegrams." He also delivered 69 Sunday evening radio broadcasts. During the Depression, Rogers's column shed light on social and political events at home and abroad. His humorous slant on politicians and the state of the economy provided a welcome lift to many Americans during those hard times.

Rogers was one of the first public figures to see trouble on the horizon. In 1928, he had written, "Wall Street is in good shape, but Eighth Avenue [where retail stores were located] never was as bad off. The Farmers are going into the Winter with pretty good radios, but not much feed for their stock."[11]

During a speaking tour he began in January 1931, Rogers raised thousands of dollars for needy Americans. While in various cities and states, he asked legislatures to develop programs that would give people work at a living wage.

Paula McSpadden Love, curator of the Will Rogers Memorial in Claremore, Oklahoma, from 1938 to 1973, speaks for many when she writes, "I contend that nothing could be written about America during the 1918–1935 period without including Will Rogers, because he spoke on the events as they happened, day by day."[12]

entered the war in 1917, President Wilson asked Hoover to head the U.S. Food Administration. In this capacity, he organized a massive food relief effort that helped to feed and house more than 10 million Europeans. Later, President Warren Harding appointed Hoover secretary of commerce.

Throughout these years, Hoover had an exemplary personal and professional reputation. In his 1922 book *American Individualism*, Hoover spoke against the maldistribution of wealth, calling for "an equality of opportunity" for all and cooperation among Americans.[13] For these and other reasons, Hoover was viewed as a practical idealist and was liked by both Republicans and Democrats. He won election easily in 1928. As Coolidge prepared to leave office, he told Congress, "The country can regard the present with satisfaction, and anticipate the future with optimism."[14] Hoover was inaugurated in March 1929. In September of that year, the stock market peaked, reaching its highest level to that date. During the previous eighteen months, stocks as a whole had tripled in price; only a few individual stocks had not at least doubled. Speculation remained high, as price dips were followed by rebounds. September and October saw more ups and downs, with a major dip on October 24. But only a few people seemed worried.

On August 10, 1929, Will Rogers had written, "The whole financial structure of Wall Street seemed to fall the other day on the mere fact that the Federal Reserve Bank raised the amount of interest from 5 to 6 percent. Any business that can't survive a 1 percent raise must be skating on mighty thin ice."[15]

The ice was soon to break. Herbert Hoover would see the first year of his presidency end in an economic free fall. Americans had a society based on money. Now, the money was about to run out.

# 2

## A Chain of Disasters

Prosperity this Winter is going to be enjoyed by everybody that
is fortunate enough to get into the poor house.[1]

—WILL ROGERS, DECEMBER 1930

Critics had pointed out cracks in America's economic structure
from time to time. For months, the stock market had been rum-
bling. On Tuesday, October 29, 1929, disaster struck.

On the morning of the Crash, about 1.5 million Americans—around 5 percent of the population—owned shares of
stock. Although stocks opened at moderately stable prices, the
sell-off began soon after the opening bell, increasing in volume as
the day went on. Much of the selling may have been triggered by
brokers who needed to repay loans and could no longer make
adequate payments on the large amounts they had borrowed. In
addition, the market may have reached the point where no new
buyers were coming in. As it stopped rising, those who were in
for quick profits would want to take their profits while they
could.

Within hours, the total value of the common stocks listed on
the New York Stock Exchange had gone down by billions of dollars. As selling continued, more people sought to get out of the
market before prices dipped further and they lost all their money.

At the Stock Exchange itself, traders screamed and pushed

each other out of the way, losing eyeglasses, shoes, even false teeth in the process. One journalist called the sounds coming from the floor an "eerie roar," while others compared it to "howling hyenas."[2] Traders rushed across the floor carrying wastebaskets full of sell orders. Orders were being filled so quickly that nobody could guarantee what price a given stock would bring.

In offices throughout America, stockbrokers watched anxiously as ticker-tape machines reflected plunging prices. The tapes were running one to two hours late, unable to keep up with the rapid activity at the Exchange. As stocks declined, brokers made more "margin calls," asking customers to send money to cover the costs of stocks they had bought, since profits had now been erased. Customers who could not cover their margin debts had to sell.

News of the mass selling spread on Wall Street. Some people entered the Exchange only to leave in a daze, trying to comprehend the catastrophe. Noisy crowds gathered outside, waiting for updates. Other people nervously paced the streets. It was rumored that several New York businessmen had committed suicide.

On that day, which became known as Black Tuesday, 16 million shares of stock were sold at a loss. Small investors who had bet their life savings on stocks lost everything. Families that had been living a comfortable or luxurious lifestyle on borrowed money now found themselves deeply in debt.

By afternoon, it was clear that this was no mere "correction" (adjustment) in the stock market. Several of the nation's most influential bankers organized a meeting at the offices of J. P. Morgan & Co. The men agreed that each of their banks would contribute $40 million to buy stocks the next day. By propping up the market in this way, they hoped to stem the panic.

The next day's headline in *The New York Times* read: "Stock Prices Slump $14,000,000,000 in Nation-Wide Stampede to Unload; Bankers to Support Market Today."

## TRYING TO RESTORE CONFIDENCE

In the wake of the Crash, political and financial leaders sought to reassure the nation. President Hoover and members of Congress told the American people that the economy was basically sound. Financier John D. Rockefeller announced, "My son and I have for some days been purchasing stock." This led comedian Eddie Cantor (who had lost money himself during the Crash) to retort, "Sure, who else had any money left?"[3]

Reports of the meeting at J. P. Morgan & Company calmed some investors, and prices on the New York Stock Exchange remained fairly stable on Friday and on Saturday, a half day on Wall Street. But on Monday, November 4, prices sank to new lows, as more people apparently decided to get out. On Tuesday, once again, millions of shares were traded, which meant that many stocks lost much of their remaining value. Corporations that had lent money to brokers, who had then lent it to clients, decided to get it back. Speculators who had bought stocks with this borrowed money received calls insisting that they repay their debts. They had to sell their stocks for whatever prices they could get.

It was another dismal week on Wall Street. Headlines in *The New York Times* reported on the continuing collapse of stock prices. Officials then ordered the Exchange closed from Thursday afternoon until the next Monday. They hoped that investors would calm down by then. Stock prices continued to slide in the days that followed. The group of bankers that had met with J. P. Morgan decided to do nothing further.

It took only two weeks to erase all the gains of the previous eighteen months. The market bottomed out in mid-November. By then, stocks had lost $50 billion, about 50 percent of the value they had had before October began.

## A Downward Spiral

Although most Americans did not own stocks or suffer direct losses during the sell-off, the Crash set off a chain reaction in the economy. It exacerbated problems already present and created new ones. Some corporations and banks that lost money in the Crash went bankrupt and shut down. Since many companies were intertwined, those linked with failing businesses went down, too, even though they had been doing well. This left more workers jobless, adding to the unemployment that had been growing all summer.

Gordon Parks, now an African-American author and photojournalist, was seventeen years old when the Depression began. He had been working as a bellboy at The Minnesota Club, an exclusive retreat for prominent men in Minneapolis. This was just one of several part-time jobs Parks held to put himself through high school. One day, Parks spotted a notice on the club's bulletin board. It said that some people would be laid off "due to unforeseen circumstances." Parks later wrote,

I read everything I could get my hands on, gathering in the full meaning of such terms as . . . deflation and depression. I couldn't imagine such financial disaster touching my small world; it surely only concerned the rich. But by the first week of November, I, too, knew differently; along with millions of others across the nation, I was without a job. All that next week I searched for any kind of work that would prevent my leaving school. Again it was, "We're firing, not hiring." "Sorry, sonny, nothing doing here." Finally, on the seventh of November, I went to school and cleaned out my locker, knowing it was impossible to stay on. A piercing chill was in the air as I walked back to the rooming house. The hawk had come. I could already feel his wings shadowing me.[4]

## Banks Fail

As a result of the Crash, banks that had been heavily involved in the stock market lost money, and some went bankrupt. Those that had lent large sums to brokers often could not collect their debts, which meant they did not have enough cash on hand for their depositors to withdraw. Some depositors lost their life savings as banks failed.

In 1930 alone, more than 1,300 banks closed. They included the Bank of the United States in New York City, with its sixty branches. With this one closing alone, the savings accounts of nearly 500,000 people were frozen. Between 1930 and 1932, 6,000 banks, mostly small ones, failed and closed. Some months saw hundreds of closings, such as October 1931, when 522 banks failed. Bank employees were among the first to lose their jobs.

Fearful men and women throughout America lined up to remove their money from banks. Some received all or part of it, but for others there was nothing. At times, bank windows shut down in their faces. People trying to withdraw their money from closed banks could be heard shouting or weeping in frustration and fear.

The deterioration of the U.S. banking system began in the rural West, then spread to major cities like Detroit and Baltimore. Isabel Lee recalls, "My grandfather was the president of a bank in Parnell, Iowa, that had to close. He sold all of his property except his house to pay back his depositors out of his own pocket. Even though it was not his fault, he never seemed to get over the shame of it."[5]

Many banks were sound, but depositors were so frightened they tried to withdraw their money anyway. To stem the panic, some banks devised ingenious plans. In West Virginia, the Bank of Morgantown was financially sound and had adequate cash assets. Its stockholders and depositors agreed to leave funds in the bank a minimum of one year, during which time the bank would close. At the end of one year, people could begin withdrawing about 20 percent of their money every three months. Depositors would receive their interest, but the bank's stockholders would not get dividends. But remedies like these were quite rare, and most depositors were left without their money.

## REDUCED CONSUMPTION

In the weeks following the Crash, orders for goods declined and inventories piled up. There was economic standstill. Companies laid off employees or reduced the number of hours people could work.

With no confidence in banks, people hoarded money at home. Many were also afraid to spend it, fearing even worse times ahead. Wealthy Americans who had lost large sums during the Crash stopped buying, so sales of luxury cars and other high-ticket items declined sharply.

There were no other consumers to pick up the slack. Most people simply had no money to spend on manufactured goods or farm products because they were unemployed. Statistics painted a grim picture: by April 1930, 3 million people were unemployed; by the end of 1930, more than 4 million. That number would soar to 13.5 million by early 1932—nearly one-third of America's labor force.

As a result, from 1929 to 1932, the national income fell from more than $80 billion to under $50 billion. Wages provided the entire livelihood of most Americans, so they could not buy goods or services, which fed the Depression. Across America, businesses closed their doors—banks, brokerage firms, shoe stores, appliance stores, clothing stores, dressmaker shops, bakeries—one after the other, as buildings became deserted.

## From Bad to Worse

Six months after Black Tuesday, more than 3 million people were out of work. Long lines of people circled the blocks around employment agencies throughout America. For most Americans, a job was the sole means of support. Many had no savings, and those who had provided for "a rainy day" had only enough to survive for a short time. Other Americans lost their savings in the bank failures that were occurring on a regular basis.

People who lost their jobs had trouble finding new ones or had to take jobs at much lower wages. Americans had less purchasing power, which, in turn, reduced the demand for goods even further, meaning more lost jobs. So the cycle continued.

Joblessness often led to homelessness. For the first time, homelessness became a widespread and growing problem in America. Without jobs, people could not make their monthly mortgage payments to the bank, resulting in foreclosures, in which banks sold the debtors' property in order to collect their debts. Some families were able to make special arrangements with banks to keep their homes. Those banks allowed them to pay less than they owed each month—for example, only the interest on the debt. People who rented homes or apartments and failed to pay their monthly rents were often evicted. A number of Americans moved in with relatives to save rent money. Those who could not find a place where they could afford to live became homeless.

Adding to these problems, natural disasters afflicted the nation. Floods in southern states led to crop failures and losses of homes and farms. In the summer of 1930, droughts in Kentucky and around the Midwest and parts of the South affected twenty-one states. As bodies of water dried up, people had to carry water to their livestock, crops, and gardens. Trains, wagons, and trucks carried water to many towns.

During the Depression, millions were ill housed and, worse, homeless. Homeless people found places to live anywhere they could, living in abandoned tenement houses, in cardboard boxes on fire escapes, in railroad stations, and on docks. In Pittsburgh, in September 1931, 1,500 people were sleeping on loading docks, train platforms, and in the doorways of buildings. In New York City, people camped out at Grand Central Station. People also moved into garages or parts of garages.

Homeless people often banded together in abandoned lots where they built flimsy shelters from discarded crates, scrap lumber, scrap metal, and cardboard boxes. As communities of these shelters sprouted all over America, people began calling them "Hoovervilles," a sarcastic reference to the man whom many people blamed for the ongoing Depression. Many thought Hoover should take decisive actions to help the needy.

These spaces were uncomfortable, as well as crowded and lacking any sanitary facilities. During cold weather, people slept under rugs for extra warmth and dressed beneath them before rising. Those who had no rugs used newspapers for warmth, often lining their walls or the insides of their coats with papers. Such newspapers were called "Hoover blankets." Other things were named for the president: "Hoover stew" was the thin soup given out at emergency kitchens; a "Hoover hog" was a jackrabbit, a tough-fleshed animal that people on the prairie ate when they had nothing else; and "Hoover leather" described the pieces of cardboard people stuffed in their shoes to replace worn soles.

People in southern cotton and tobacco areas suffered, especially sharecroppers and farmers who raised only one kind of crop. During that first year of the drought, aid from Washington and the Red Cross saved some farmers from starvation and prevented further loss of livestock. But farm prices dipped lower because people were not buying.

Throughout America, many people did not have enough to eat. Some merely cut back on their daily meals, but others scoured garbage cans for scraps just to stay alive another day. Those who had no place to turn stood in "breadlines" waiting for whatever charity could afford to give them. One day you might get thin soup, a slice of bread, and coffee; another day a cheese sandwich and coffee; or baked beans with toast and coffee. The food was sometimes so meager that men went to one breadline after another. As more and more people lined up and joined the ranks of the needy, local charities were fast running out of money.

## No Government Relief

Where were desperate people to turn? In those years, there were no government-sponsored unemployment insurance, welfare, food stamps, or other programs for people in need. Local communities often aided orphans, widows, or people too sick or disabled to work. But these programs were few in number and limited in scope. People in trouble were expected to help themselves, relying on family and friends if need be, or seeking help from private charities. The idea that people should handle problems on their own was an old tradition in America, where independence and "rugged individualism" were prized.

As the Depression deepened, private charities and local governments were swamped with requests for food, clothing, fuel, and other assistance. Yet they had even fewer resources than usual, since contributions had plummeted. Some charities even received letters asking them to return large donations that had been made the previous year by wealthy people who were now in debt.

Individuals and community groups tried to bridge the gap. A

During the Depression, getting through school, not to mention pursuing higher education, was a struggle. To keep schools open, teachers often gave up their pay or worked for less money. College students whose families had fallen on hard times had to leave. Some colleges opened cooperative dorms, where students did the chores and prepared their own meals to reduce expenses.

Around the country, some children were ashamed to attend school because of their worn-out clothing or because they lacked shoes. In Houston, Texas, some boys told a government worker they would not go out in the trousers they had been given, made of black-and-white striped material, because then everyone would know they were on relief.[6] Other children quit school to help out at home or on the farm, or to take a job that would help support the family.

The education system in some places broke down. Wyoming was among the states where schools were spread out and located near urban areas. Parents whose children attended high school had been accustomed to boarding them in town. But as droughts and swarms of crop-destroying grasshoppers hit that

New Yorker named William H. Matthews operated the Association for Improving the Condition of the Poor, which raised $8 million from financiers and millionaires by December 1930. His organization gave the unemployed jobs in public works.

In Philadelphia, Philip H. Gadsden, president of the Chamber of Commerce, urged his "Buy Now" project. Gadsden asked people to contribute 15 cents a day to fund jobs for the unemployed, who would be paid wages of $6.25 a day. The Lions Club and other groups helped to raise the money. But such programs could help only a small portion of those in need.

region, hundreds of families had no money to pay boarding expenses, so young people stayed home. Nor could they find any jobs to pay their own way.

Describing conditions in rural Georgia, journalist Lorena Hickok wrote, "If there is a compulsory school system in the state, it simply isn't functioning. It can't. The children just can't go to school, hundreds of them, because they haven't the clothes. The illiterate parents of hundreds of others don't send them. As a result, you've got . . . hundreds of boys and girls in their teens down here in some of these rural areas who can't read or write."[7]

Those schools that remained open often cut back in various ways. Moses Crutchfield, a student in Greensboro, North Carolina, during the 1930s, recalls, "Believe me, it was a different world in those days. . . . The story of our class [which graduated in 1937] as it made its way through high school reflected that fact. There were not trips to Washington or even to Raleigh. Greensboro High had been kicked off the list of accredited schools by the Southern Association of Secondary Schools mainly because the term was for only eight months."[8]

## HOOVER RESPONDS

Most historians believe that President Hoover and his advisers did not grasp the severity of the Depression and thought it would run its course like the economic slumps of the past. Hoover believed that the unemployment that followed the Crash would end after a few months. He continued to claim that the economy was basically sound. Using the word *depression* was also his idea. Hoover thought the word *panic*, used to describe economic crises of the past, would frighten Americans.

Hoover was not indifferent to the suffering around him but could not seem to stem the tide. He worked with national leaders and experts from different fields to find solutions and supported measures that are supposed to allay economic downturns: he asked business owners not to cut wages and to keep investing in their businesses, he lowered taxes, and he urged people to buy goods rather than hoard their money. Economists praised Hoover, saying that he was doing far more than a president had ever done during an economic depression. Hoover's limited response was also based on the fear that people would stop relying on themselves and their own initiative, depending instead on government charity.

In November 1929, the president proposed a tax cut which some critics termed "rich relief" because it benefited some large corporations and wealthier Americans. Hoover hoped that with lower taxes they would spend more and hire more people. But when the legislation was passed, no noticeable gains resulted.

By winter 1930, Hoover was asking Congress for $150 million to aid the unemployed, an unprecedented appropriation. It had become clear that private agencies and local communities could not handle the problem. Hoover also signed bills that allocated $300 million in loans to farmers, drought relief, and emergency construction that would employ some of the jobless. He initiated a voluntary program through which bankers could help the weaker banks, using $500 million in government aid. But this program failed, possibly because there were no penalties if banks did not take part.

Hoover was roundly criticized for signing the Hawley-Smoot Tariff Act in 1930, which aimed to protect the market for U.S. goods by placing high tariffs on imported goods. More than 1,000 economists urged the president to veto it.

As a result of Hawley-Smoot, European nations were unable to continue making payments on their war debts, and U.S. investments in Europe were curtailed. European nations experienced a financial collapse in 1931, at which time they had to devalue their currencies. There had been signs of some recovery in the American economy in 1931, but worsening conditions in Europe, along with the collapse of many European banks, killed it.

Meanwhile, factories continued to shut down or cut back, farmers kept going bankrupt, and more businesses closed their doors. The Empire State Building in New York City, taller than any in the world with its 102 stories, was completed in 1931. It remained mostly empty.

On December 30, 1931, Will Rogers wrote, "Well the old year is leaving us flat, plenty flat. . . . It's took some of the conceit out of us. We have enjoyed special blessings over other nations. And we couldn't see why they shouldn't be permanent. We was a mighty cocky nation. . . . We had begun to believe that the height of civilization was a good road, bath tub, radio and automobile. . . . I think the Lord just looked us over and decided to set us back where we belonged."[9]

# 3

## From Panic to Despair

Last year we said: "Things can't go on like this." And they didn't—they got worse.[1]

—WILL ROGERS, 1932

As the Depression deepened, millions of Americans experienced unexpected deprivation or real poverty, either quickly or over a period of time. For some families, the Depression meant giving up luxuries or conveniences, such as their telephone service or summer vacations. Others spent year after year battling to stay alive. For many individuals, the struggle began with job loss, then the loss of savings, credit, and possessions. People lost their pride and, sometimes, their hope.

As breadwinners became unemployed, their lives often followed a terrifying pattern. Other family members sought work, usually without success. Food became scarcer and plainer; people grew thin and wore shabby clothing and shoes. Embarrassed by their appearance, children often would not go to school.

People borrowed money from families and friends and ran up rent and food bills until they could borrow no more. They sold or pawned their belongings and found smaller, cheaper housing. Eviction might come after a year of not paying the mortgage or when their debt reached $1,000 or so.

Some families moved in with relatives, sleeping in dining rooms and living rooms, often three or four to a bed. Those with nothing left went on relief. With luck, they might be able to survive and stay together. Sinking into poverty, people felt anger, frustration, and despair, blaming themselves, blaming the government, or wondering just who or what *was* to blame. How could their lives, and the lives of so many others, have gone so wrong?

## UNEMPLOYED, UNDERPAID

Job loss—the worst fear for most Americans—might come suddenly, with a "pink slip" (dismissal notice) inside a pay envelope. Or it might drag out over a period of weeks and months as a factory went through a slowdown, in which workers were cut back to a few days of work every week, followed by wage cuts before the final blow of being let go.

All over America, factories let workers go as orders dried up. The nation's auto plants had produced 4.5 million automobiles in 1929; by 1932, they were making only 1.1 million. Automaker Henry Ford had pledged to keep his factories running. But, in 1931, he shut down his Detroit plants, and 75,000 people lost their jobs. Suppliers, middlemen, sellers, and others in the auto industry also suffered.

From 1930 to 1932, there was so much competition for jobs that wages declined, with many people making half or one-fourth as much as they had in 1928. Store clerks received $5 a week, and some factory workers made only 25 cents an hour. A top secretary might make $10 a week, the same amount a household servant earned in a month.

People looking for work would line up for potential employers at 5 A.M. even in midwinter, hoping for something, anything, to earn a few dollars. Lines often stretched along several blocks, with people standing three or four abreast. Many applicants did not reach the door of the building until hours later. Usually only married men with families were hired.

While hard times brought out the best in some people, they brought out the worst in others. Since labor was cheap, managers could ignore labor laws and exploit workers. Children toiled in sweatshops, earning less than $8 a week in some cases for 100 hours of labor, even in states where child labor had been outlawed.

Sometimes advertisements described inviting, well-paying jobs for credit or business managers or buyers—positions that did not exist. When they arrived, applicants were told the job had been filled and they were offered a job that paid "on commission," so they would only earn money after selling a certain amount of goods. Some employment agencies charged people a week's pay for getting them a job. Then those workers were sent to a company that would fire them after the first week so they wound up with no pay at all, a scheme that benefited only the agency and the company. Other employment agencies sold people special clothing or equipment for jobs that never materialized.

With so many seeking work, employers could be choosy, setting their own terms. They found ways to discriminate against job applicants, some of them irrational, and many—based on age, sex, religion, race, or marital status—that would be illegal today. For instance, a nursing school rejected an applicant because she had crooked teeth. A teacher was denied work in New York City because she weighed 182 pounds and, according to examiners, might have trouble moving fast during a fire drill.[2]

Job hunters also had trouble keeping a neat appearance that would help them get a job. As one woman would write to First Lady Eleanor Roosevelt, "The unemployed have been so long with out food-clothes-shoes-medical care-dental care etc.—that we look pretty bad—so when we ask for a job we don't get it. And we look and feel a little worse each day . . ."[3] A jobless man in Oregon commented, "We do not dare to use even a little soap when it will pay for an extra egg or a few more carrots for our children."[4]

Those who had additional trouble finding jobs included people of color, newly arrived immigrants, and women. Married women had an especially difficult time. Between 1930 and 1931, a survey of 1,500 school districts showed that 77 percent would not hire married women. Sixty-three percent had fired women teachers who were married. A total of 82 percent of Americans agreed with this idea, telling pollsters in 1936 that a married woman should not work if her husband had a job. As late as 1939, companies were still withholding jobs from women.[5]

As they gave up hope for full-time jobs, some people did piecework, such as sewing buttons on cards, or tried door-to-door selling. A number of others, including veterans, sold apples on city streets. There had been a bumper crop of apples in the Northeast in 1930, and growers invited unemployed people to buy and resell them. A box of 72 apples cost $2.25, and each apple could be sold for about 5 cents—or more if the customers were generous. After spending 10 cents for carfare to pick up the apples and 10 cents for bags, the profit per box was $1.15. The apple sellers became a poignant symbol of hard times.

## MORE PROBLEMS FOR FARMERS

The Depression brought worse times to the farm. As prices fell, many farmers burned corn and other grains for fuel rather than sell them at 15 to 31 cents a bushel, less than these grains cost to produce.

Taxes on farmland had been calculated during the "good times" of the twenties, and remained at those same rates during the Depression. Payments on equipment still came due, too. During the Depression, farmers had even less money to pay their debts, and banks were too strapped to wait for payment. People who lost their farms might also face a lifetime of debt afterward, since there might still be debts to pay even after the farm was sold.

In some places, as farms were put on the auction block, friends and neighbors might attend the auction and set up a hangman's noose nearby, a sign that nobody should try to buy the farm. As the auction began, those people would offer a few dollars for the property, threatening anyone who tried to bid higher. These low bidders then returned the farm to its owner at the end. Banks became resigned to getting whatever low prices they could.

There were angry confrontations between farmers and law enforcement officials in rural areas, sometimes leading to bloodshed. Desperate farmers resorted to threatening bankers and kidnapping sheriffs to prevent foreclosures on farm property where tax and mortgage payments were in arrears. Bitter farmers in Iowa and Nebraska organized strikes as part of the Farm Holiday movement. They refused to ship crops to market and picketed railroads, overturning trucks and dumping milk, to enforce their boycotts. By 1932, some politicians feared that unrest in the Midwest might lead to outright revolution.

## NOT ENOUGH FOOD

While farmers had surpluses and were destroying food crops they could not sell at a profit, other Americans were starving. During the depths of the Depression, in the winter of 1932, New York City hospitals reported ninety-five cases of starvation, with twenty deaths, as well as thousands of cases of malnutrition.

Malnutrition was widespread. Relief workers found people subsisting for weeks on potatoes, beans, salt meat, corn bread, white bread, rice, and coffee. In Danbury, Connecticut, a woman and her small daughter, found sleeping under a canvas strip, had eaten only apples and wild berries for five days.[6] Families of four sometimes had 30 to 50 cents a day for food. Many tried to fill up on stale bread, which could be had for 3½ cents a loaf.

Desperate people foraged through garbage cans outside restaurants and hotels or went to docks, searching for discarded, spoiled vegetables they might turn into soup. Raw potato peelings were also made into soup, or eaten plain. People begged.

It is impossible to know exactly how many died or became ill because they lacked the right nutrients or enough protein during these years. In many cases, people grew weak from eating poorly over a long period of time. Some were too sickly even to look for work. Others, if they finally found jobs, were too weak to work.

Hearing about the plight of people in New York City, the people of the Cameroun, in Africa, collected $3.77. They sent it to city officials to be used for "the relief of the starving."[7]

## ON THE MOVE

Thousands of homeless people took to the roads. About 2 million Americans roamed the country, including 250,000 young people. The men were known as hoboes, and they were joined by young people, most over the age of nine or ten, who had left home for various reasons. Young people might leave home so their parents would have fewer mouths to feed, but some left because poverty had broken up the family and they did not want to live in foster homes or orphanages. Often, young people traveled in groups, with girls joining boys for protection.

On the road, people hitched rides or hopped aboard freight trains when guards were not watching to get from place to place. Once in a new location, they tried to find work and food, sometimes on farms, picking grapes or other crops. Hoboes begged if all else failed.

It was a difficult, unpredictable life. People went without baths, wearing dirty clothing, and often did not know when they would eat again or where they would sleep. At times, they were arrested, but at least that meant a bed for the night. They could usually find a bowl of soup, some beans, or a peanut butter sandwich at local relief centers run by churches, the Salvation Army, the Volunteers of America, or local communities.

To help each other, hoboes left messages in the form of pictures drawn with chalk or crayon on sidewalks, kitchen doors, and walls. "Hobo signs" told where to find food and kind homemakers and warned about dangerous dogs and places where hoboes were unwelcome. An x beneath a smiling face showed that a doctor would treat people for free, while a circle with an x in the center showed homes where hoboes could receive food. A semicircle with a dot underneath showed that police were watching for hoboes.

Many wanderers headed for the Southwest. Some made their way to the beaches of California. There they could camp year-round, find firewood on the shore, and fish for food and gather shellfish—crabs, mussels, abalones, blue cod, rock cod, perch, and sea trout. They tended gardens, raising onions, kale, potatoes, lettuce, turnips, carrots, and Swiss chard.[8]

Others continued to roam. The despair of many was expressed in a poem written by an eighteen-year-old in Ohio:

> *We are the men who ride the swaying freights,*
> *We are the men whom Life has beaten down,*
> *Leaving for Death nought but the final pain*
> *Of degradation. Men who stand in line*
> *An hour for a bowl of watered soup,*
> *Grudgingly given, savagely received.*
> *We are the Ishmaels, outcasts of the earth,*
> *Who shrink from the sordidness of Life,*
> *And cringe before the filthiness of Death.*[9]

## SEEKING RELIEF

As the Depression went on, the rolls of the needy increased greatly: About 7,400 families sought public relief in Boston in

1929; that number rose to more than 40,600 in 1932. In Chicago, by 1932, 40 percent of the workforce (700,000 people) were out of work. The needy now included people who had once been comfortably middle-class: professional and businesspeople who found themselves out of work. Newspapers reported more cases of children starving to death, particularly in stricken areas like Appalachia.

Distribution centers were set up at railroad stations, in vacant lots, and on street corners. People lined up for blocks to receive the goods. Officials in Cleveland doled out farm surplus butter, potatoes, and cabbage to the needy.

Yet relief hardly allowed people to subsist. A weekly allotment might be $15.40 for six people, which broke down like this: food—$7.75 and 70 cents for milk (10 cents per quart per day);

clothing—$1.80 (30 cents per person a week); coal for kitchen range and heat—$2.50; rent—$1.40; gas—65 cents; electricity—60 cents.[12]

When relief funds ran low, families received less, sometimes only $2 to $3 a week. They used this meager allotment to buy fuel and food. That left nothing for rent, clothing, shoes, medicine, transportation, or health care.

Relief for needy families might take the form of weekly food vouchers. On the voucher were printed the foods approved for buying. Banned were ice cream and newspapers; people were not allowed to use relief money for movie tickets or church donations.

When cities ran out of funds, relief stopped. By mid-1932, about one-third of all Americans were known to be out of work, a possible total of 20 million. Thousands literally faced starvation. During the spring of 1932, hundreds of families in Philadelphia, Pennsylvania, endured an eleven-day period when the city had no funds to distribute. To survive, people ate stale bread, watery soup, and scraps found in garbage pails. Infants were fed water mixed with flour.

"Going on relief" was a devastating blow for people who had been used to supporting themselves. Over and over during the Depression, relief workers found that people wanted jobs, not charity. Humiliated at the thought of being "on the dole," people waited until they were desperate before asking for help.

Author Russell Baker later recalled the pain his family felt in 1933, compelled to go on relief when his widowed mother could not find work. Taking the wagon he used when delivering newspapers, his family walked several blocks to the relief center, where men handed them food, all in unmarked cans, or in bags showing that it came from the government:

There were huge cans of grapefruit juice, big paper sacks of corn-meal, cellophane bags of rice and prunes. It was hard to believe this was ours for no money at all . . . My wonder at this free bounty quickly changed to embarrassment as we headed home with it. Being on relief was a shameful thing. People who accepted the government's handouts were scorned by everyone I knew as idle no-accounts without enough self-respect to pay their own way in the world. I'd often heard my mother say the same thing of families in the neighborhood suspected of being on relief. These, I'd been taught, were people beyond hope. Now we were as low as they were.[13]

## CHARITY RUNS OUT

From the beginning of the Depression, private charities had been providing help. President Hoover had called upon them to ease the suffering, and such groups did what they could. In Chicago and other cities, teachers gave food to hungry children in their classes and used their own money to buy school supplies. Chicago and other cities went bankrupt because landlords who could not collect rent were then unable to pay their property taxes.

The Red Cross was doing relief work in many states, but this organization was designed to deal with short-term emergencies, not years of unmet needs. Public and private relief activities continued to operate, but most had exhausted their resources after the first winter of the Depression.

Fund-raisers were held for the needy. They included movie weeks, supper dances at fine hotels, sporting events, and performances by people from the entertainment industry. In New York City, $1.3 million was raised by collecting door-to-door throughout the city. New York City employees gave over 1 percent of their salaries to support a fund run by the police that gave food to starving families. But by early April 1932, New York had run out of funds and was turning down 700 families a day who asked for relief. Clearly, private resources were not capable of meeting such widespread needs.

## Angry Citizens

Frustration grew among the hungry and homeless and those who feared they would soon join these ranks. People who had never broken the law turned to stealing. There was violence and rioting in cities and rural areas throughout the nation.

Hunger led people to break the law. On March 19, 1930, in

---

### ∼ THE BONUS MARCHERS ∼

In 1932, some World War I veterans living in Portland, Oregon, decided to march to Washington, D.C. After the war, Congress had voted the men bonuses of about $1,000 each, scheduled to be distributed in 1945. The men, unemployed and out of money, needed the bonuses now. Walter W. Waters, an unemployed former army sergeant, was chosen to lead the march and present a petition to President Hoover.

Called the Bonus Expeditionary Force, the marchers pledged to maintain order and discipline and banned drinking and disorderly conduct. To get to Washington, they walked, rode freight trains, and took rides from friendly strangers. Reading about the march, other veterans came, too—from Illinois, New York, California, Louisiana, until every state was represented and some wives and children had joined the group.

Numbering about 25,000, they reached the nation's capital and set up camps, chiefly on marshy land across from the Anacostia River. Superintendent of Police Pelham Glassford, himself a veteran of World War I, was convinced the marchers intended no harm. He helped them get food from army field kitchens.

On June 15, 1932, the House of Representatives authorized immediate payment of the bonuses. However, two days later, the Senate defeated the Bonus Bill. Veterans waiting outside the Senate building were upset but remained calm. After singing the patriotic song "America," they returned to their camp.

New York City, more than a thousand men were standing in a breadline when two trucks full of baked goods arrived. The men seized the food, which was being delivered to a hotel. In July 1931, 300 unemployed men in Henryetta, Oklahoma, threatened local storekeepers unless they gave out food. In Oklahoma City, twenty-six looters were arrested for taking food in grocery stores. Looting also occurred in Minneapolis, Detroit, and other cities.

In January 1932, a march on Washington was led by Father

Some remained in Washington, having nowhere else to go, and were still there in July. Superintendent Glassford sent what food he could, even using $1,000 of his own money to help the veterans. Hoover refused to meet with them, and Congress adjourned without passing the Bonus Bill.

The administration was uneasy about the Bonus Marchers' continuing presence and decided that they threatened security. Federal troops under Army Chief of Staff Douglas MacArthur were told to clear the camps. Tanks and cavalry troops arrived with bayonets and tear-gas bombs to oust the men, women, and children, who were told to gather their belongings and leave within an hour. After the confrontation ended, it was found that a baby born in camp that summer had died of tear-gas inhalation. Two Bonus March veterans died after being shot by police earlier in the day.

About the marchers, one congressman had said, "These ragamuffins cannot remain here indefinitely. They have no business in Washington. They don't belong here."[14] But to many people, the Bonus Marchers did have a right to see their president. Critics viewed the attack on their camp as an outrage, another sign that the administration cared little for the average American or the suffering caused by the Depression. The attack increased public resentment toward President Hoover.

James R. Cox, pastor at St. Patrick's Church in Pittsburgh. For weeks, Father Cox had collected money for the food and gas the marchers would need. Between 10,000 and 18,000 men undertook the trip, which was conducted in an orderly manner. The governor of Pennsylvania gave them shelter overnight as they assembled.

Once in Washington, the group notified the chief of police that they had arrived and what they planned to do. They slept in cars, trucks, and the National Guard Armory. The army at Fort Meyer distributed apples, doughnuts, and coffee for breakfast, then the men marched, eight abreast, waving small U.S. flags. At the Capitol, they handed out signed petitions that declared people had a "God-given right to work" to Senator John Davis and Representative Clyde Kelly of Pennsylvania. Cox led the Pledge of Allegiance, and the marchers sang three songs. The men then presented a petition to President Hoover and asked for a $5 billion bill that would fund public works programs, relief, and aid to farmers. The petition said that gift and inheritance taxes, affecting the wealthy, should be raised to 70 percent. There was no immediate response from the president and neither Hoover nor Congress set up any public works programs.

A few weeks later, Detroit was the scene of much distress. By 1932, relief bills in Detroit totaled $2 million a month. In March, about 3,000 men staged a hunger march after the unemployed stopped getting relief payments. The Ford auto plant had moved outside the city limits, so the company no longer paid taxes there.

Outside the Ford plant in Dearborn, Michigan, the marchers, who included many members of the Communist Party, asked to present a petition. When they refused orders to leave the area, police launched tear gas. In retaliation, the jobless men threw rocks and chunks of ice. They were finally quelled with blasts of frigid, high-pressure water and gunfire. Many people were wounded; a sixteen-year-old and three others died. On their coffins, the workers hung red signs that read: "Ford Gave Bullets for Bread."[15]

## Reaching the Depths

By the start of 1932, economic indicators showed that the nation's problems were severe and would not end soon. Stock prices had continued to fall after the Crash, so that by July 8, 1932, the prices per share of all the common stocks listed on the New York Exchange added up to $58. Stocks that had once sold for over $100 a share were often going for less than $1 per share in 1932.

Realizing that stronger measures were needed, Hoover signed legislation creating the $2 billion Reconstruction Finance Corporation (RFC) on January 22, 1932. It was authorized to distribute money to banks, insurance companies, agricultural associations, and railroads, as well as to give states money to meet the needs of their residents. These loans were made in secret so that people might regain confidence in banks without knowing the aid was really coming from the federal government. However, some operations of the RFC were reputedly dishonest and much of the money did not reach individuals in need.

Animosity toward the Hoover administration escalated. Many people made wry jokes or criticized the president while some threatened violence against the government. Observers feared that if the government did not take drastic action, and soon, the nation would sink even further and might experience a bloody revolution.

# 4

## *The Poor Got Poorer*

### *Minorities and Other Special Groups*

For millions of folks it is a very hard time. There is nothing that they personally can do to help their position. Their living has always been made by working, by holding an honorable job, but there is no job to hold.[1]

—WILL ROGERS, 1932

"Last hired, first fired," goes an old saying about the long struggle for access to employment by African Americans and other minorities. The Depression worsened their plight, since millions of others, mostly whites, vied for the same jobs. Minorities, including Mexican Americans, often faced outright hostility. Out-of-work whites feared Mexican Americans would get scarce jobs or offer to work for lower pay.

Rural poverty, an ongoing problem in America, reached crisis proportions during the Depression. Low farm prices, droughts, and dust storms ruined the livelihoods of thousands, causing numerous farmers and their families to migrate west. Conditions for people in mining regions also deteriorated.

## AFRICAN AMERICANS

In his book *Hard Times*, Studs Terkel quotes an African-American man from Chicago who said, "The Negro was born in depression. If you can tell me the difference between the depression of today [the 1950s] and the Depression of 1932 for the black man, I'd like to know."[2] Black Americans had long endured the hardships and deprivation that many Americans sampled for the first time during the Depression.

By the 1930s, many African Americans had left the rural South for northern cities, where they hoped to be treated more equitably and find better jobs. Some were making progress and were able to make ends meet when the Depression hit. Author Milton Meltzer describes a family with six children that moved to New York from Georgia. When the father became ill, they relied on the income of the mother, who had always held a job, and the oldest son, who left college at age nineteen to work full-time. After ten years, the family had managed to save $2,000, which they used to buy a home in Queens, New York. But when the Depression hit, both the son and mother lost their jobs and they could no longer pay the mortgage. The bank foreclosed on the property—sold it to pay the debt.[3] Like many others, this family was forced into smaller and bleaker housing, in ever more run-down neighborhoods.

Throughout the nation, African-American families made up a disproportionate share of those on relief, because they had the most trouble finding work and had been poorer to begin with. In Chicago, four out of ten relief clients were black. In Pittsburgh, African Americans made up about 8 percent of the population, but by early 1931 about 40 percent of the unemployed were black men.

With jobs so scarce, it was easier to exploit people desperate to work. African Americans had to put up with more threats and injustices than whites in order to keep the jobs they had. Some foremen asked for bribes from those who wanted to avoid being fired or demoted. Many employers also expected a great deal more work for the same or less pay. Featured in the February–March 1932 issue of *Opportunity* magazine were ads for live-in housekeepers to cook, care for children, and do all the laundry and cleaning for as little as $6 a week.[4]

## BLACK CITIZENS PROTEST

Although black Americans were often penalized in the past for protesting, many courageously spoke out during the Depression. Black veterans of World War I were among those who traveled to Washington, D.C., in 1932 with the Bonus Expeditionary Force.

African Americans joined hunger marches and labor protests in various cities and opposed evictions or unfair treatment of individual citizens. Horace Cayton, a black journalist and sociologist who was the grandson of Hiram Revels, a senator from Mississippi during Reconstruction, reported some of these events. In September 1931, Cayton was eating in a Chicago restaurant when he saw a group marching down the street protesting the eviction of a black family, one of many evictions that occurred during the early 1930s. When a policeman confronted the crowd and told them to disperse, a young man said, "All we want is to see that these people, our people, get back into their homes. We have no money, no jobs, and sometimes no food. We've got to live some place. We are just acting the way you or anyone else would act."[5]

Cayton watched the crowd expand, and various people spoke, including an eloquent African-American woman. He wrote, "It [the crowd] had grown bigger now and many white faces were seen. The [police] stood and listened. I don't believe that there was any one there who was not touched by the talk. I don't believe that there was anybody there, white or black, who did not in some degree face the same situation that she was so vividly describing."[6]

Many people moved from place to place looking for work. In January 1930, future author/photographer Gordon Parks, a native of Kansas, packed a cardboard suitcase, stuffed two dollars in his pockets, and hopped on a train bound for Chicago. For the next two years, he would wander from place to place, taking whatever jobs he could find, living in cheap, sometimes unspeakably filthy, rooming houses.

Finally, in 1933, he and a friend joined the Civilian Conservation Corps (CCC) program set up by the Roosevelt administration and were stationed at Camp Dix, in New Jersey. Parks later wrote, "We planted millions of trees, fought the Dutch elm disease, built fishponds, fed wildlife, cleared tremendous areas of beach and camping ground . . . But when July came the depression still choked the country, and I knew that it would still be around when our time was up in October. . . . the employment offices, park benches and hobo villages would still be full."[7]

## TENANTS AND SHARECROPPERS

Southern blacks suffered as much as or more than those in the North. Most were sharecroppers or tenants—farmers who paid for the right to work another person's land. Sharecroppers paid by giving the owner half the crops they raised, while tenants paid rent. Often whole families worked all day, every day, to eke out a living. They raised cotton and different kinds of food, such as corn, used to feed stock animals, and potatoes, peas, and sorghum for themselves.

During the Depression, there were nearly 9 million such farmers, slightly more than half of them black, the others white. Most lived on $150 to $250 a year, earnings they might not even see if they were indebted to the landowner. Seven or more people might struggle to survive on that sum. They lived in flimsy shacks without plumbing, heating, or even windows, and subsisted on sowbelly (a kind of pork), cornmeal, and weeds.

Dropping farm prices during the twenties and thirties made the lives of these poor farmers even more harsh than in previous decades. The price of cotton fell from 21 cents a bale in 1927 to a low of 8 cents a bale. Those farmers who had been borrowing against future crops to pay rent and taxes fell even farther behind.

Journalist Lorena Hickok traveled throughout America to study conditions and send reports to the Roosevelt administration. She wrote about tenant farming in the rural South:

> Their whole system has been built up on labor that could be obtained for nothing or for next to nothing. When their slaves were taken away, they proceeded to establish a system of peonage that was as close to slavery as it possibly could be and included Whites as well as Blacks. That's all a tenant farmer is—or has been, up to the present time—a slave. . . .

> The tenant lived on the landlord's farm, in a house owned by the landlord. During the slack season, when there was no work, the farmer took care of him—"furnished" him as they call it down here—either by buying his food and giving it to him, or by giving him credit at a store he owned. The tenant never had any money—never could "buy himself out." The property owner was his lord and master, could impose any terms he liked.[8]

Through various means, some dishonest, landowners kept tenants and sharecroppers in debt. They were often overcharged for the seed, tools, farm animals, and housing supplied by landlords. Many tenants could not read, so they could not determine if the owners were keeping accurate records. One tenant who tried keeping track of his own accounts said,

> I tried keeping books one year, and the man [owner] kept worrying me about it, saying his books was the ones he went by anyhow. And nothing you can do but leave. He said he didn't have no time to fool with books. He don't ever give us no rent notes all the

time. They got you cause you have to carry your cotton to his mill to gin and you better not carry your cotton nowhere else. I don't care how good your cotton is, a colored man's cotton is always second- or third-grade cotton if a colored man sells it. The only way you can get first prices for it is to get some white man to sell it for you in his name. A white man sold mine once, and got market price for it.[9]

## APPALACHIA

For years, the people living in the mountainous areas of Appalachia had depended on wild game and small plots of corn and beans for their food. Later, they had sold timber for cash, but went to work as miners during the late 1800s.

As mines closed down and work dried up during the Depression, people in Appalachia became destitute. Whole communities turned to public relief, but relief was often halted for lack of funds. People would stand silently at the door of the relief office, most unable to read the notice that had been posted, waiting for someone who could explain what it meant. Some starving people had to beg.

In Harlan County, Kentucky, thousands of people had no income at all. Caroline Bird writes, "They lived on dandelions and blackberries. The women washed clothes in soapweed suds. Dysentery bloated the stomachs of starving babies. Children were reported so famished that they were chewing on their own hands. Miners tried to plant vegetables, but they were often so hungry that they ate them before they were ripe."[10]

Dysentery was only one of the diseases that ran rampant. Tuberculosis, typhoid fever, diphtheria, and diseases caused by nutritional deficiencies, such as pellagra, were found throughout the region. Like others, the mining families did not have enough heat or clothing. Some were so ill clothed they could not even leave their cabins. Seeing one such case, a local investigator commented, "The women folks in [that] place hain't got no clothes at all. Even their rags is clean wore out and gone."[11]

President Hoover sent $2,500 of his own money to aid people in Harlan County. Others, mainly members of the Rockefeller family, also sent donations. But the need was deep and ongoing. As Lorena Hickok observed,

> In Middlesborough [Kentucky] Saturday night I heard of a miner's widow with six children who had had nothing at all to eat that day and had no prospects of getting anything the next day either. At the Continental hotel in Pineville I was told that five babies up one of those creeks had died of starvation in the last ten days. . . . They're neighborly folk, down there in the Kentucky mountains and mining camps. Those who have share with those who haven't. Even, I was told, to the last string bean.[12]

In one area, a relief worker persuaded grocers to make up packages of cornmeal, lard, sugar, and coffee, enough to last a family for a week, for 85 cents each. The grocers agreed to give out a free package for each one purchased for a community. The relief center raised money from private sources to fund this project, but again, such measures helped only for a short time.

Some mines began opening up again in 1933. At one regional welfare office in West Virginia, a state field representative reported that men had come into the office, jubilant, asking to be removed from the welfare rolls because they were going back to work. However, the joy was short-lived for many. The representative said, "A day or two later they began drifting back bewildered and frightened. They'd passed the age limit [which was set at about forty-five]. There was no work for them. Some of them cried like children."[13]

While the policies of the Roosevelt administration would bring food and some help to the region, the deeply entrenched poverty of Appalachia would persist for decades after the Depression. During the 1960s, it would move two presidents—John F. Kennedy and Lyndon B. Johnson—to take stronger action.

## MIGRANTS FROM THE DUST BOWL

As if the Depression were not bad enough, the 1930s brought severe droughts and dust storms to the Great Plains. During the late 1800s, pioneers had settled in Nebraska, Oklahoma, Texas, Arkansas, and Missouri to work farms from about forty to eighty acres large. Many of them were called "dry farms" because they lacked irrigation systems or other sure means of bringing water to the land. The region was notorious for the droughts that came periodically.

Nevertheless, during times of more rain, farmers went farther into the Plains. They cultivated millions of acres of land in order to raise more wheat and other grains, for which there was increased demand during World War I. Called "sodbusters," the farmers had to dig up dense prairie grasses and break through the tough earth to sow their crops. What they did not know was that these grasses held the soil together, retaining enough moisture to prevent erosion.

Dependent on rain, people on the Plains and in parts of Texas, Kansas, and New Mexico were devastated by the drought that arrived early in 1932. This drought was to last for five years, wreaking misery in part of the Texas Panhandle, southeastern Colorado, and the northwestern strip of Oklahoma, a region that became known as the Dust Bowl. Day after day, farmers scanned the sky for any sign of clouds as their crops shriveled and died. David J. Wilson, who grew up on a farm in eastern Nebraska, recalls, "One summer the corn grew only as large as my thumb. After days of no rain, huge cracks, big enough for me to run around and hide in, opened in the ground."[14]

Winds, sometimes reaching fifty miles an hour, swirled dirt

and dust through the air. Clouds of dust concealed the sun, even at midday. Dust seeped under doors or windows that had been lined with wet towels, covering floors with layers of dirt. It coated farm animals, killing those whose nostrils and air passages became clogged. People covered their faces to avoid choking when they were outdoors and hid in storm cellars to escape the ugly "black blizzards." Winnie Everett recalled, "There were times it got so dark from the dust storms we went to meet our kids at school to bring them home."[15]

As the topsoil was carried off, the red clay that remained on these lands was no good for farming. What meager crops could be raised were devoured by grasshoppers, which thrive in hot, dry weather, as well as hungry pheasants, rabbits, and other animals. R. K. Everett recalled, "We planted seeds . . . but they didn't grow. . . . It stayed dry so long we had to give up our cattle because there wasn't enough for them to eat."[16]

In addition, farm prices had been falling since the late twenties. By 1932, about 1,000 families a week were being evicted from their farms. Most Oklahoma farmers were unable to raise enough wheat, corn, or cattle for even a meager living. They resorted to selling livestock or machinery or borrowing more money. To live, they killed and ate jackrabbits, along with biscuits and beans.

Many families left their land to search for work. During those years, some 1 million people migrated west—the largest migration in U.S. history. The migrants included some African-American families, although the vast majority were whites from Oklahoma and Arkansas. Most headed for the San Joaquin Valley of California, hoping to find jobs in the fields. They had heard that California was a land of boundless orchards and fields of fruits and vegetables, where growers paid good wages. California growers had advertised for workers by distributing handbills that said: "Plenty of Work—High Wages! Needed Now! Start Work Right Away!"[17]

Moved by the plight of the "Okies" from the Dust Bowl who left home in search of a better life, California-born author John Steinbeck lived among them and grew to understand their ways and special problems. To the families he met and spent time with, he became known as "Migrant John."

In California and Oklahoma, Steinbeck saw thousands living in huge, sprawling camps, with no work available, no hope. He completed a series of articles about the migrants, then began work on his novel *The Grapes of Wrath.* Steinbeck wrote,

> *There are five thousand families starving to death over there, not just hungry but actually starving. . . . In one tent there are twenty people quarantined for smallpox and two of the women are to have babies in that tent this week. . . . The death toll of children by starvation in our valleys is simply staggering. . . . Funny how mean and how little books become in the face of such tragedies.*[18]

Steinbeck was appalled to find that in many camps, though children and others were starving, landowners would not give them the surplus crops. Some even set fire to these crops while hungry migrants looked on. Steinbeck called this "a crime that goes beyond denunciation."[19]

*The Grapes of Wrath* portrayed the migrant experience as lived by the Joad family. The impact of Steinbeck's novel in revealing the problems of migrants has been compared to what Harriet Beecher Stowe's *Uncle Tom's Cabin* did to raise consciousness about slavery.

The trip to California was an arduous journey, some 2,000 miles long, that included hills and a 143-mile stretch across the Mojave Desert. There, temperatures could reach 120 degrees and no gas stations were available to provide fuel or parts for a broken car. The trip to California might take as long as six months.

Along the way, families ate bacon and biscuits made from lard and flour they had brought along, as well as weeds, wild berries, and anything they could pick or catch. Some survived on carrot stems, fruit pits, even coffee grounds.

Upon reaching the coast, disappointed migrants found that the growers had enticed a surplus of workers in order to keep wages low. Many workers spent backbreaking hours in the fields for just 25 cents, which kept them in poverty and terrible living conditions. Some found no work, while others who did were frequently victimized.

Unable to move on because there was no work or gas, they pitched tents or lived in cardboard squatter communities, in camps of ramshackle huts, or in their cars. Many survived by eating boiled cabbage and corn bread day after day. The damp cold and unsanitary conditions led to health problems. Children died of tuberculosis, dysentery, pneumonia, and other diseases. Some hospitals refused to accept the migrants as patients and left them to die. In addition, local people ridiculed the shabby, uneducated migrants, sometimes calling them "dumb Okies," and signs like "Okies, Go Home!" often confronted them. Migrant Mae McMasters later told author Jerry Stanley, "People acted like we was dirt under their feet."[20]

In 1936, the Chavez family, which included five children, piled their belongings in an old Chevrolet and drove around Arizona and California looking for field work. The whole family would work for a week and receive only $5 or $10. Sometimes the crew pusher (a person who specialized in finding workers to do cheap labor) would claim that he had not received any money from the grower and skip town before paying the workers.

Cesar Chavez, who later organized migrant workers and founded the United Farmworkers Union of America, recalled these experiences: "We would work after school. Sometimes we wouldn't go. 'Following the crops,' we missed much school. Trying to get enough money to stay alive the following winter, the whole family picking apricots, walnuts, prunes. We were pretty new, we had never been migratory workers. We were taken advantage of quite a bit by the labor contractor and the crew pusher."[21]

The migrants would later have some relief in 1937 when the federal government began building camps in the San Joaquin Valley, providing better shelter and living conditions. The one-room tin cabins and tents on wooden platforms, hot showers, and flush toilets were a great improvement. Families paid $1 a week rent, but those who could not afford it could work instead by doing chores around the camp. A child's breakfast cost one penny. While living in the camps, people found jobs in nearby towns or on farms.

At one such camp, every Saturday night people gathered in an auditorium built from scrap lumber to sing and listen to people play instruments. These kinds of activities developed a sense of community that helped migrants withstand the rejection that came from the people around them.

Although poor people obviously suffered even more than others during the Depression, millions of Americans joined their ranks for the first time, and their attitudes about poverty were shaken. People began to question the old ideas that the poor must be "too lazy to work" or "unwilling to take care of themselves." Now, those who had always prided themselves on independence and hard work were poor, too.

# 5

## *Living Tight*

We will just about have to save ourselves accidentally. That's the way we stumbled onto prosperity.[1]

—WILL ROGERS, AUGUST 1931

While many Americans experienced dire poverty, millions of others had just enough to get by. The average family income, about $2,300 in 1929, fell to $1,600 or less in 1932.[2] Families that had managed on $1,500 now tightened their belts further to support themselves on $660 ($55 a month), a typical salary for a city schoolteacher, for example. On this amount, a family could survive if no serious health problems or other crises occurred.

People were resourceful. The old saying "Use it up, wear it out, make it do, or do without" was never more true than during the Depression. Families moved in together to save rent money; some people took in boarders. Women sold their baking, sewing, and knitted goods. They canned garden produce and bought day-old bread or made their own. They sewed their own clothing and made their furniture, sometimes using orange crates for storage and shelves.

People saved fuel by using the oven only when it was full. They looked for things that could be had free, such as borrowing books from the library or sharing newspapers and magazines. They collected coal that fell off trains around the railroad tracks and chunks of ice that fell from ice delivery trucks. Farmers sold their produce door-to-door to avoid the costs of shipping or middlemen. People took to bartering. It was all part of what people called "living tight," getting along day by day in tough times.

## EATING TIGHT

The most basic problem for most families during the Depression was getting enough to eat. Food budgets were cut to the bone, and homemakers looked for ways to serve their families wholesome meals at the lowest possible cost. People ate a lot of the same foods, finding numerous ways to cook potatoes, cornmeal, and noodle dishes, baking batches of buttermilk biscuits and pancakes, and stretching small amounts of meat. They added more bread and milk when there was little else to go around.

One immediate way to save money was simply to cut down on the amount of food a family ate. A can of soup might be dinner for four people. (By the 1930s, there were twenty-one kinds of Campbell's soup.)[3] Other meals, often just before the paycheck or relief check was coming, consisted of cocoa or coffee with bread.

Simple meals were the rule for most families. Ida Lewis recalls, "We might have boiled or baked beans with a little salt pork or bacon for dinner. With biscuits, that was it. We had a lot of macaroni and noodles, sometimes with some cheese sauce or gravy. Few people had much meat."[4]

An egg had to last for two meals, recalled Lonnie Goddard who lived on a farm in West Virginia. "I'd have the white for breakfast and put the yellow on corn bread for lunch at school."[5]

Food could be stretched in many ways. Some people softened a pound of butter, then mixed it thoroughly with canned milk so that it lasted for several weeks. Ground meat was mixed with bread, oatmeal, and other items to make it go farther.

Yet people still had the urge to be creative and make life as pleasant as possible. Homemakers shared recipes that were cheap but filling and tasty. Radio shows dispensed money-saving hints and described menus and dishes listeners could try at home. Major food companies, such as General Mills, sponsored these popular programs and used them to promote their products.

Farm families often had more to eat and more variety. Thelma Moeller of Delta, Colorado, recalls, "We had plenty to eat but not much else. It was often just a large pot of vegetable or potato soup, made with water and served with homemade bread. Mom always made 18 or 20 loaves of bread a week and we had plenty of hot biscuits made by Dad for breakfast."[6]

Lena Galchick recalls the importance of the family garden and annual canning of food during her childhood in Flushing, Ohio:

We were able to survive because of our mother. She was always frail but tough, never giving up. A few years earlier when work was good, my folks bought a double lot. The home was built on one lot, and the other was used for planting. They grew every vegetable that could be planted. We ate the food in the summer and canned the rest. Over five hundred jars would be put up. We would pick wild raspberries and blackberries to make into jam, jellies, canned fruit for pies. With the tomatoes, we would make catsup, tomato paste, tomato sauce, chili sauce. The end of summer would be a very busy time. If the food wasn't put up for winter, there just wouldn't be any food to eat. During the hot days of August, it would be very hot to stand in front of the big black iron stove. We would go to the nearby field for dandelions, watercress, mushrooms, and other edible greens. . . . We raised some chickens for eggs and to eat.[7]

Lillian Galchick remembers, "Mom would send me uptown to the meat market to buy 10 cents' worth of soup meat on a bone. There was enough to grind up for meatballs and some left on the bone to make soup. We had a general store where we bought all our groceries and every two weeks when Dad got paid we would pay off the bill. We would be all excited on that day because when the bill was paid they would give us a bag of candy. You could get ten pieces for one penny."[8]

## KEEPING UP APPEARANCES

With no money to buy new clothing, people wore more hand-me-downs and mended everything. Adult clothing was cut down to be made over for children. Old coats could also be relined with blankets. A worn-out sweater could be unraveled and the yarn reknitted into several pairs of mittens. People knitted their sweaters, caps, scarves, socks, gloves, and capes.

Dish towels and dishcloths were made from the cloth sacks that held twenty-five pounds of flour from the relief center, and so were dresses, skirts, and blouses. Families made sheets and pillowcases from feed sacks after bleaching away the print. Shirts could be made by sewing two layers of burlap together.

Some people made clothing from batches of remnant fabrics—the pieces left over after large pieces have been cut—which were sometimes ordered from the Sears Roebuck catalogue. Remnants could also be found in bins at the local "piece goods" store.

Shoes were often a problem, since few people could make shoes themselves. Many people wore their shoes only outside the house to prevent wear and tear, or they carried them as they walked to church. Rubbers could be worn in town to hide holes, and people stuffed cardboard inside their shoes where holes showed. Worn-out soles were sometimes replaced with cut pieces of old tire rubber or even cardboard.

During the Depression, women still wore hats throughout the year and liked them to look attractive. Instead of velvet, they bought practical felt hats, which were more durable. If a new hat was beyond the budget, they found ways to fix an old one by freshening the trim with feathers, lace, buttons, and ribbons from the scrap basket.

While "making do," families tried to maintain their standards and their pride. Lena Galchick says, "No one suspected how really poor we were because we always were clean and well groomed. Since Mom sewed, we wore nice dresses, jumpers, and blouses. Our house was always clean, the lace curtains always crisp. Our table always had a tablecloth and cloth napkins."[9]

People eating at the charity soup kitchen in Flushing, Ohio, were also treated respectfully, she recalls: "They would set up long tables, neatly set with regular china plates and flatware. The place was always overflowing with mostly schoolchildren."[10]

## BARTERS AND TRADES

As people ran out of money, they began trading for goods and services. Doctors, dentists, and lawyers were given chickens and other food in lieu of fees; at times, their patients or clients did yard work or household repairs. Some people used furniture, paintings, silverware, or family heirlooms to pay their bills.

Caroline Bird writes, " 'Swaps' began to appear in newspapers. 'Man's overcoat in good condition, for slide trombone, piccolo, or French horn.' At Ohio State University, students used cigarettes for currency; in some places they were scarce because local merchants did not have cash to pay the stamp taxes. . . . Colleges took eggs or even sacks of coal in exchange for tuition."[11]

People organized cooperatives where they could trade goods and services. To make exchanges easier, many barter systems issued scrip—"money" they made themselves that could be redeemed for other things. In Lansing, Michigan, for example, a farmer who gave vegetables to the exchange received scrip he could use as part payment for his wife's funeral. The undertaker redeemed the scrip by having another person in the cooperative paint his hearse.

In Seattle, Washington, unemployed people cut timber for fuel, harvested unsaleable fruits and vegetables, and caught fish in exchange for the services of doctors, seamstresses, barbers, and others.[12]

## FAMILY LIFE

Divorce rates were lower during the Depression years, falling 43 percent between 1928 and 1933. Analysts believe that people could not afford to divorce as often during those times or that, for some, hardships brought them closer. Birth rates also fell, from 21.3 live births per 1,000 population in 1930 to 18.4 by 1933.[13] Many couples were fearful of bringing more children into the world. During these same years, however, information about birth control became more widely available, and that may also have been a factor in declining birth rates.

For many families, hard times showed the value of teamwork and cooperation. People had to pull together to survive, and children helped with the work of the family without expecting an allowance.

Often, families spent more time together, reading or just talking. In his memoirs, journalist Russell Baker recalled,

> Unlike the movies, talk was free, and a great river of talk flowed throughout the house, rising at suppertime, and cresting as my bedtime approached before subsiding into a murmur that trickled along past midnight, when all but Uncle Charlie had drifted off to bed, leaving him alone to reheat the [coffee] pot, roll another cigarette, and settle down with his book.[14]

Baker and his mother and sister lived in a small home with his uncle Allen, Allen's wife and two children, and two other grown uncles. Much of their talk centered on politics, in America and throughout the world. Baker recalls that the grown-ups "expressed . . . congenial contempt toward business, labor, government, and all the salesmen of miracle cures for the world's ailments. Communists were 'crackpots' and 'bomb throwers.' Father Coughlin and Huey Long were 'rabble-rousers.' The German-American Bund with its Nazi swastikas 'a bunch of sausage stuffers.' "[15]

They talked about other things, too—movies, philosophy, morals, baseball, music, family history. Baker writes, "It was common for the poorest household to contain a large dictionary, for conversation was a popular Depression pastime and Americans were passionately interested in words."[16]

Lillian Gobitas was growing up in Minersville, Pennsylvania, during the 1930s. Her father operated a small grocery store, and the family, including Lillian and her brother, lived upstairs. Gobitas later said, "It was hard in Minersville during the Depression years. I remember Dad had a little account book for the bills that people ran up, all yellow and old. Some people never paid, but he never went after them. When the WPA and relief finally came along, it was quite a help. Those measures were very good."[17]

Gobitas felt that her family was lucky in some respects: "At least we had food. Everything was do-it-yourself. We learned to sew, and make do with lots of hand-me-downs. It was not awful. We were really a jolly family. While we worked we would listen to those old radio shows."[18]


## GOOD TIMES

People of every era like to have a good time, and during the Depression, they found ways to do it with little or no money. For example, a game called "Handies" could be played for free. The players placed their hands in different positions, with different motions to represent a thing or action. Others tried to guess what they were doing. The board game of Monopoly came out during the Depression and gave people the vicarious chance to "wheel and deal" as property owners. People also played chess, checkers, and card games.

Roller-skating and Ping-Pong could both be enjoyed with little expense. According to the Department of Commerce, in 1931, Americans bought 2.7 million pairs of roller skates. Adults were encouraged to skate in order to stay fit. Audiences also saw popular film stars Fred Astaire and Ginger Rogers roller-skating in the movie *Shall We Dance?*

Although the Depression was nearing a peak early in 1931, 70,000 football fans turned out for the Rose Bowl game in its seventeenth year, when Washington State played for the Western division against Alabama. In many communities, sports lovers organized softball and baseball teams and played anytime the weather was decent. Friends gathered at one another's homes after the games for an inexpensive meal—perhaps corn bread with maple syrup—followed by card playing.

For entertainment, the DePietro family of Flushing, Ohio, joined other families once a week at someone's home for a party. There, a band made up of a violin, guitar, and accordion provided entertainment. The adults drank coffee and homemade wine, and peanuts, the only food, were served.

Children found ingenious ways to create toys from bits of paper, wood, and scraps. Boys made scooters out of scrap lumber, part of an orange crate, and discarded roller-skate wheels.

From discarded magazines and catalogues, girls made paper dolls that could provide many hours of fun. They cut out pictures of families and found clothing in the catalogues that fitted them. Using homemade flour-and-water paste, they attached the dolls to pieces of old cardboard boxes.

During the Depression, enterprising, hardworking young people looked for ways to earn money. Those in rural areas might earn a few pennies a pound picking beans for a nearby canning factory. Young people took different odd jobs or delivered newspapers or sold magazines, such as the gossipy magazine *Grit*, the *Woman's Home Companion, Collier's,* and *The Saturday Evening Post.*

Most people could not afford to pay up front for a whole year's subscription. By selling subscriptions or extra copies of a magazine, a boy or girl could earn what were called "brownie points" and "greenie points." They accumulated these points until they had enough to choose prizes from a special book. Prizes included items of clothing, books, and small toys.

Fred Von Gunten, a doctor's son, grew up in Berne, Indiana.

## Simple Gifts

Birthdays and holidays were celebrated in simpler ways as families tried to enjoy them with little expense. A birthday gift might be a dime, some fruit, a few comic books, or a simple toy like a few marbles.

For the Fourth of July, many families stayed home, since there was no gas to drive anywhere for a picnic. But lemonade, popcorn, and homemade ice cream might be special treats for the day.

At Christmas, people made do as they did during the rest of the year. Gifts were simple and often homemade. Children might sharpen a feather to make a quill pen for a parent or loop scraps into a mat or pot holder. Parents might make a sled, wooden pull-duck, or other toy. They might cut up their own clothing to fashion skirts or shirts for their children or knit them scarves.

After the Depression hit, his father's patients stopped paying cash for their care and said, "Charge it" or gave him only a small part of the fee.[19] Or they gave the doctor eggs, chickens, chunks of beef, and other commodities. Once, a patient gave Dr. Von Gunten a saxophone—"which is why I played the saxophone in high school when I really wanted to play a trumpet," Fred Von Gunten recalls.

With their newspaper routes, he and his brother earned $2 apiece each month, which their parents urged them to save "for a rainy day." While he was in high school, working as a janitor, office boy, and clerk in a bookstore after class, Von Gunten was able to earn about 10 cents an hour. One Christmas, knowing his father did not have money to buy new license tags for their car, he used his savings to give them to his father as a gift that was deeply appreciated.

One family started their "10-cent" Christmas tradition during the Depression. Each person bought a 10-cent gift for someone else in the family. Key chains, new cake pans, a tiny container of bath salts, a small tool, a cigar, fresh dish towels— these were some of the items that could be had for a dime. The family enjoyed the tradition so much that they continued it in later years, increasing the amount to a dollar by the 1960s.

Homemakers saved up bits of sugar to make a batch of fudge or other candy or baked treat. At night they popped corn, perhaps some they had raised themselves.

The Depietro family of Flushing, Ohio, had no money for gifts during the Depression. The highlight of the Christmas holiday was going to church, followed by a bountiful meal prepared with great care: clear broth, homemade macaroni, roasted chicken and potatoes, and salad. For dessert, there were fried doughnuts filled with fruit preserves.

Because gifts were the exception, greeting cards became more important during the Depression. The card industry had been around since the early 1900s, when companies called Hall Brothers (later Hallmark Cards) and American Greetings were formed. They created greeting cards for Christmas and birthdays.

Some Depression-era cards made light of poverty and other difficulties, while others spoke optimistically about the good times that lay ahead. In one of these humorous cards, an elderly man was featured in the picture, and the lines read:

> *This isn't what I'd like to send!*
> *Ain't being poor a crime!*
> *Perhaps I'll have a million bucks*
> *to send to you next time!*

Many people who lived through the Depression years say that despite the hardships, it was not all bad, or even a terrible time to grow up. Says Dolly Ott of Merrimac, Wisconsin, "I wouldn't exchange my Depression years on the farm for anything. One learned how to help himself and survive."[20]

## LOOK AND LISTEN

All over America, people watched the 1932 presidential campaign with more interest than usual. Democratic candidate Franklin Delano Roosevelt had decided to crisscross the nation by rail, visiting every region to talk with citizens and local officials. He called this his "look, listen, and learn" campaign. In the cities, Roosevelt saw people in rags begging on street corners, and long lines outside soup kitchens. He saw midwestern farms where farmers burned corn for fuel because, at 15 to 31 cents a bushel, it was cheaper than coal and too unprofitable to raise. He saw the migrant camps in the West. All around, there was a shabbiness—in people's appearances; in run-down homes; in the farms, barns, and fences that needed repairs.

And everywhere, thin, hopeful faces stared at Roosevelt as crowds gathered to hear him speak. Many people greeted the chance for a new leader with enthusiasm. Another reason for Roosevelt's popularity was that Americans knew he had faced hard times himself. Born to an aristocratic, wealthy family, Roosevelt had enjoyed a life of privilege, fine schools, and vacations in Europe. But in 1921, at age thirty-nine, Roosevelt was stricken with polio, a disease that attacks nerves that control muscle function. The muscles in his legs were paralyzed, and doctors said he would never walk on his own again. Roosevelt spent months working to walk a few steps with crutches, then with heavy metal leg braces. In public, a family member, friend, or aide walked or stood beside him for physical support.

Elected governor of New York in 1928, Roosevelt had supported progressive reforms to help the needy and unemployed. He favored old-age pensions, unemployment insurance, conservation, and public works projects. During his campaign for president, Roosevelt spoke of aggressive welfare and reform plans—a "New Deal"—which he viewed as the only way to save America's free-enterprise system. He promised aid for farmers and more government regulation of businesses, the stock market, and utility companies.

Election results showed that Americans favored Roosevelt's New Deal. He carried all but six states and won with a total of 22,821,857 popular votes to Hoover's 15,761,841. "Roosevelt Winner In Landslide!" declared *The New York Times* on November 9, 1932.

For many, the change in leadership came not a moment too soon. By the time Roosevelt was inaugurated, foreclosures on mortgaged homes had reached the staggering number of 1,000 a day,[21] and four-fifths of the states had suspended banking operations. One-third of the American people were now poor.

# 6

## *Fighting Fear Itself*

We are all getting ready for the new deal. We don't know what
kind of hand we will get, but we want it even if it's just deuces.[1]
                                    —WILL ROGERS, FEBRUARY 1933

Thousands of people gathered in Washington, D.C., for the
March 4 inauguration of Franklin Delano Roosevelt—or "FDR"
as he was often called. An estimated 200,000 to 300,000 visitors
were in the capital. Hotels overflowed, with people sleeping in
cots in the halls and lobbies, while others slept in school gymna-
siums, church basements, and the Pullman cars of passenger
trains. The rest found spots on park benches and in libraries and
movie theaters. The Red Cross distributed coffee and doughnuts.

The theme song of the Roosevelt campaign had been
"Happy Days Are Here Again," and Americans fervently hoped
this would prove to be true. Things had never seemed bleaker. By
the time FDR took office, there was a widespread mistrust in the
currency itself. Coins were in demand, since paper money was
thought to have dubious value. People who tendered large bills
for bus rides, newspapers, telephone calls, and other things might
be refused change. Banks in Detroit and many other places would
not cash paychecks for municipal workers.

The banking system had weakened since the November election. Most of the nation's banks were now closed, as was the New

York Stock Exchange and the Chicago Grain Exchange. Rumors and panic worked together to cause depositors to withdraw money even from sound banks. Sometimes, depositors were robbed as they walked home after withdrawing their money. A police officer in Brooklyn, New York, said, "All the crooks have to do is watch and see who comes out of the bank and then follow him. It's a mess."[2]

## A STIRRING ADDRESS

As he planned his inaugural address, Roosevelt knew that his words carried great weight and would set the tone for his presidency. He hoped to lift people's spirits and inspire confidence, at the same time showing that he understood the grim conditions facing America.

As Inauguration Day dawned, around 650,000 spectators began lining Pennsylvania Avenue and looking for standing room in Capitol Square, where the ceremony would be held. The crowds were delighted when rays of sun broke through the cloud-littered sky during the ceremony. Throughout the nation, millions turned on their radios to hear the president.

In a resonant, firm voice, Roosevelt spoke words of reassurance, saying, "This great Nation will endure as it has endured, will revive and will prosper. So, first of all, let me assert my firm belief that the only thing we have to fear is fear itself—nameless, unreasoning, unjustified terror which paralyzes needed efforts to convert retreat into advance."[3]

He admitted that with so much unemployment and poverty gripping the nation, "only a foolish optimist can deny the dark realities of the moment. . . . This Nation asks for action, and action now." And Roosevelt promised to treat the situation "as we would treat the emergency of a war. . . . We must act and act quickly."[4]

Although the president did not give all the details, he briefly outlined plans for curbing unemployment and improving agricultural and industrial markets. The administration, said FDR, would move quickly to reduce foreclosures and unify various relief activities. It would develop utilities, transportation, and communications systems of a "public nature." Roosevelt also pledged to take immediate measures to provide for a sound currency and to safeguard the banking system. Together, he declared, the nation and its leaders would mount "a disciplined attack upon our common problems."[5]

The administration faced a daunting task: to lift the spirits of a disheartened, frightened people, then set in motion programs to deal with the crises and promote economic recovery. The wide array of programs that composed FDR's New Deal were controversial and continue to be so to this day. They created federal jobs and massive public welfare programs. But few legislators opposed Roosevelt, who had enormous public support. Besides, they were willing to try almost anything that might relieve the Depression.

## ATTACKING MONETARY PROBLEMS

On Inauguration Day, Roosevelt asked his secretary of the treasury, William Woodin, to create legislation to regulate banking. The next day, Roosevelt declared a national "bank holiday." All of the banks still in business would close until further notice. Roosevelt issued a second executive order banning people from hoarding or exporting gold. Some wealthy citizens had been buying gold and sending it out of the country in case the U.S. dollar collapsed.

The president then convened an emergency session for Congress, beginning March 9. Thus began the dynamic period in the Roosevelt administration that would be known as the "Hundred Days." A huge amount of legislation was drafted and set before Congress. A diverse group of people representing both parties would design Roosevelt's New Deal, and his closest advisers would become known as his "Brain Trust." Republican Raymond Moley later said, "We had forgotten to be Republicans or Democrats. We were just a bunch of men trying to save the banking system."[6]

Later, the Emergency Banking Act of 1933 would put commercial and investment banking into separate spheres. Bankers

---

### ∼ FIRESIDE CHATS ∼

On March 12, FDR held his first "fireside chat," addressing the American public by radio. Roosevelt began by saying, "I want to talk for a few minutes about banking . . . I want to tell you what has been done in the last few days, why it was done, and what the next steps are going to be."[7]

Speaking in a clear, reassuring way to Americans, the president explained why he had ordered the bank holidays and how that would prevent another "epidemic of bank failures."[8] The president said that Americans could once more have confidence in their banks and could make deposits without fear.

The Sunday-evening fireside chats became a regular part of the Roosevelt years. By 1933, about 16 million families, half of the population, owned a radio. Those who did not own radios would join friends or relatives to hear their favorite shows or important news. Radio was therefore an excellent way for the president to keep in touch with the American people and to explain his policies. Each broadcast began the same way, as the President said, "My friends . . ."

Roosevelt's message evidently inspired confidence, because deposits exceeded withdrawals when the nation's banks were reopened on March 13. Three days after the "chat," the stock market reopened to the largest one-day rise in its history. During that week, the ticker tapes in brokerage offices throughout America carried a message from the New York Stock Exchange: "Happy Days Are Here Again."

could no longer float securities using depositors' money. Deposits would also be insured through the Federal Deposit Insurance Corporation (FDIC), which continues to protect deposits today.

In March, the Securities and Exchange Commission (SEC) was formed to regulate stock market practices and limit the amount of credit that could be used for speculating. Safeguards were put in place to protect investors and prevent people from manipulating stock prices, abuses that had exacerbated the Crash.

On May 25, the Truth-in-Securities Act was passed. It gave the Federal Trade Commission (FTC) power to regulate how new stocks and bonds were marketed to potential customers. Since that time, each new stock issued must be accompanied by a complete and accurate statement of the company's financial status and future prospects.

## HELPING A STRICKEN NATION

Besides banking legislation, FDR had other plans to rescue the nation. Borrowing from the Hoover administration, Roosevelt kept the idea of the Reconstruction Finance Corporation (RFC), expanding it greatly. He asked the RFC to buy stock in banks and to lend banks money to increase their working capital. New corporations were developed under the RFC to handle mortgages and credit, aid farmers, and develop electricity in rural areas. Between 1932 and 1941, the RFC lent more than $15 billion to large and small businesses.

Improvements in each area of the economy bolstered other areas. As railroads, banks, and insurance companies benefited from these measures, they had a better cash flow and could begin to repay RFC loans they had used during previous years. Some companies also resumed paying dividends to their shareholders.

While programs to build the economy were put in place, the administration began sending federal aid to the needy and unemployed. Congress passed the Federal Emergency Relief Act (FERA) with an initial appropriation of $500 million. It was directed by Roosevelt's friend Harry Lloyd Hopkins, an energetic, Iowa-born New York social worker. During his first days on the job, Hopkins authorized payments to bankrupt states, municipalities, and welfare agencies. Commenting at a Senate appropriations hearing on the need for *immediate* action, Hopkins said bluntly, "People don't eat in the long run. They eat every day."[9]

## "NEW DEALERS"

Hopkins was just one of many dedicated people who came to work for the New Deal. Roosevelt was known for his willingness to try new ideas and to consider various opinions and proposals, from both older experienced people and younger ones, men and women. Some of those who came to Washington had grown up poor and understood Americans who were suffering. Others had been born affluent like FDR himself but had seen enough poverty to develop strong social consciences.

One of the most experienced "New Dealers" was Marriner S. Eccles, a successful banker and businessman from Utah. Eccles had testified early in 1933 before a Senate Finance Committee exploring solutions to the Depression, at which time he declared,

An economic age 150 years old has come to an end. The orthodox capitalistic system of uncontrolled individualism, with its free competition, will no longer serve our purpose. We must think in terms of the scientific, technological, interdependent machine age, which can only survive and function under a modified capitalistic system controlled and regulated from the top by the government.[10]

Eccles and some prominent economists, such as Briton John Maynard Keynes, believed that a government should spend money during hard times and conserve money when the economy is strong. In this way, a government would increase the purchasing power of citizens and the demand for goods, thus boosting employment. Impressed with Eccles's practical, coherent approach, Roosevelt appointed him to the Federal Reserve Board.

Among the young professionals who came to work for the new administration was David A. Morse, a twenty-six-year-old labor lawyer and graduate of Harvard Law School. He later said of FDR, "Somehow in his fireside chats and his articulation of the problems that confronted the country, he inspired us as young people to reach out to help."[11] Another Roosevelt fan was a young schoolteacher and future president named Lyndon B. Johnson, head of the National Youth Administration in his native Texas.

Journalist Kenneth Crawford later said, "Suddenly, Washington was alive. The White House became the hub not only of the United States but of the world. The people who were brought in were exciting. . . . We felt that something was being accomplished. We felt a part of it."[12]

As the New Deal took shape, glimmers of hope appeared here and there. On March 14, just eleven days after Roosevelt's inauguration, A. P. Giannini, the head of the Bank of America in California, decided to reopen his bank, which was in a sound financial position. Giannini personally visited branches of the bank, talking with staff and bank customers. His actions boosted morale in the business community.

That same day, the administration called for the repeal of the Eighteenth Amendment, the constitutional amendment which had made it illegal to buy, sell, or manufacture alcoholic beverages in the United States. An immediate amendment to the Volstead Act, which had been created to enforce the Eighteenth Amendment, legalized the sale of beer, and later, the Twenty-first Amendment to the Constitution was passed, legalizing alcohol once again. The end of Prohibition meant that organized criminal networks could no longer profit by "bootlegging" activities.

## SOMETHING FOR YOUNG PEOPLE

By 1933, there were about 15 million young people between the ages of sixteen and twenty-nine in America. For many, the Depression had killed their dreams. Thousands were crisscrossing the country looking for work. A few, especially in large cities, turned to crime to survive.

Roosevelt devised several large programs for youth. The National Youth Administration (NYA) helped about 1.5 million young people stay in high school by giving them community jobs. The NYA also made it possible for more than half a million to get through college.

One of the most popular New Deal work programs was Roosevelt's Civilian Conservation Corps (CCC). The CCC was under several departments—Labor; Interior; Agriculture; and War, since the Army built and ran the camps. The Corps was open to young men between ages eighteen (later changed to seventeen) and twenty-five (later changed to twenty-eight) who were single, jobless, healthy, and needy. Local relief agencies enrolled people for terms of six months, which could be renewed to two years. A person promoted as a leader could stay longer.

The first CCC worker was enrolled on April 7, 1933. By July, there were 274,375 young men working and living in 1,300 camps.[13] They were paid $30 a month, with from $22 to $25 of this amount being sent home to their families. Recalls Wayman Wells,

> There were 30 boys from my county in Arkansas who went into the CCC the same day in 1936. We took a train west from Little Rock, and they called our names when we stopped at Clarksville. It was about midnight. They put us on a truck and hauled us to a

camp in the woods at the end of a dead-end road, in rugged country. It just worried me. I was 17 and scared of most everything. . . . We were all poor, hardly anybody had been away from home before.[14]

During the nine years of its existence, 2.9 million young men served in the CCC. Most joined at age eighteen and a half and served, on average, nine months. Sixty percent came from farms or small towns. Most had not finished high school, and their checks were supporting from three to four other family members. Enrollment peaked in September 1935 with 502,000 men in 2,514 camps.

About 200,000 African-American men worked in CCC. As was typical of the U.S. military in those years, there were segregated companies for whites and blacks. There were also Native Americans and veterans of World War I in the Corps. Often, Native Americans were assigned to work projects in their communities. The Roosevelt administration passed laws ending the forced assimilation policy the U.S. government had followed in the past. Under that policy, Native Americans were told, and often coerced, to abandon their cultures and religions and assimilate—adopt white ways.

Early CCC camps contained tents. Later, barracks were built to house between forty and fifty people each. Other buildings included a mess hall, recreation hall, officers' quarters, a school for night classes, and a latrine and bathhouse.

At the site, work crews supervised by the U.S. Forest Service worked on building and conservation projects with saws, shovels, sledgehammers, and axes. A typical day began at seven-fifteen and ended at four, with a break for lunch, which might be beans and applesauce served at camp. Unaccustomed to three hearty meals a day, many of the men appreciated the oranges, bananas, and breakfasts of ham, eggs, sausage, and potatoes. There were dishes called SOS and slumgullion, with fish on Friday and chicken on Sunday.

Organized sports programs at CCC camps included boxing, baseball, and basketball. The men played cards, Ping-Pong, and music in the evenings, some having brought their own instruments. Men could bring dates back to camp only at chaperoned events.

Education and vocational training were strongly encouraged. Between 1938 and 1939, about 8,500 CCC servicemen learned to read and write. Others continued their educations, taking classes in various subjects, from the elementary through high school levels.

Some enrollees later recalled unfriendly treatment from local people, including signs that said "No CCC Allowed." "I think people in general looked down on us," said Carl Denoff of West Virginia.[15] In other places, CCC corpsmen felt more welcome. Some "CCC-ers" married local women they met while at camp.

## AID FOR FARMERS

With the Agricultural Adjustment Act (AAA), the administration launched a multifaceted attack on farm problems. Directed by Henry A. Wallace, the programs aimed to increase farm prices to bring the income of farmers more in line with the income of other Americans. Since farm surpluses had led to lower prices, the AAA suggested paying a cash subsidy to farmers for *reducing* their production.

To help farmers keep their homes, land, and equipment, the Farm Credit Administration united existing farm credit agencies under one organization, directed from a central location. During the next two years, the FCA refinanced nearly 25 percent of the nation's farm loans. The Frazier-Lemke Farm Bankruptcy Act enabled some farmers who had lost their land to regain possession. In 1935 Roosevelt pointed out that farm income had risen from $5.3 billion in 1932 to $8 billion.

## "I'VE GOT A JOB": PUBLIC WORKS

For millions of people, the best news was that they could go back to work. The large Public Works Administration (PWA) received an appropriation of $3.3 billion for various projects— irrigation, dams, and reclamation—throughout America. Eventually, workers in PWA projects built Boulder Dam (now Hoover Dam), the Triborough Bridge in New York City, hundreds of hospitals, water supply works, schools, university facilities, and more than fifty military airports throughout the nation. Other projects included civic buildings and auditoriums, roads, highways, and sewage systems.

Such projects benefited industries throughout the nation— the steel mills of Pennsylvania and Ohio, the cement industry of the Mississippi Valley, the lumber industry of the Pacific Northwest, the nation's transportation network, and of course, the construction industry.

On April 10, Roosevelt asked Congress to set up an ambitious PWA program called the Tennessee Valley Authority (TVA). The TVA gave the federal government control over the Muscle Shoals electric and nitrogen plant, which had been built with tax money on the Tennessee River during World War I.

Directed by Arthur Morgan, Harcourt A. Morgan, and attorney David E. Lilienthal, the TVA would provide farmers with low-cost electric power. Control of the river would also make it possible to lessen flood damage and limit soil erosion in the region. Numerous people would be hired to build dams, fertilizer plants, and soil control stations.

Electric companies opposed the TVA bitterly, fearing that it might lead to lower power rates and more government control over their whole industry. But the TVA legislation was passed in

May. Roosevelt believed that rather than regulating power rates, the government could set a good example through the TVA. He called it a " 'yardstick' for the cost of power."[16]

A new program was launched on May 6, 1935. The Works Progress Administration (WPA), the largest of all the work relief projects, was expected to operate until 1938 but continued until 1942. It employed some 8.5 million Americans. Besides building roads, bridges, buildings, parks, and playgrounds, workers in these projects provided many useful services, working in schools, hospitals, libraries, and public health departments.

The WPA also funded educational programs for the public and supported work by writers, scholars, artists, historians, photographers, actors, and musicians. Without these projects, much of the nation's literary and artistic productivity would not have been possible during these lean years.

The Civil Works Administration (CWA) was set up during the winter of 1933–1934 as a temporary work relief program until the PWA began operating fully. People who began working on the program felt an immediate lift, according to government social service workers. Although wages were only about $15 a week, it was more than many had been living on, and they preferred working to welfare. A man in Alabama told one government representative, "When I got that [CWA identification] card, it was the biggest day in my whole life. At last I could say, 'I've got a job.' "[17]

As people began receiving paychecks, sales of groceries, clothing, shoes, and other items increased, boosting the economy in numerous communities. The CWA was highly praised, with the Literary Digest calling it "a courageous experiment on a heroic scale."[18]

During the Hundred Days, another meaningful event took place. In May, a new group of Bonus Expeditionary soldiers arrived in Washington, D.C. There were thousands of men, some emaciated with hunger, torn between despair and hope. This

~ FRANCES PERKINS: OPENING A DOOR ~

As FDR's secretary of labor, Frances Perkins became the first woman Cabinet member in history. Perkins was born in 1882 to a well-to-do family in Boston and worked among the poor as a teacher and social worker. A fighter for social welfare causes and for women's rights, she shocked some people by keeping her maiden name after marrying Paul Wilson in 1913.

Perkins was deeply moved by a tragedy she witnessed on March 25, 1911. Then an officer of the New York Consumer's League, she was walking on that Saturday afternoon near Washington Place and Greene Street. A fire broke out in the Asch Building, which housed the Triangle Factory. Hundreds of garment workers were trapped inside as elevators broke down and the one fire escape fell apart. Firemen's hoses could not reach the burning top floors. In the end, 146 workers, mostly young women, died in the blaze or from jumping to the ground trying to escape.

Perkins later said, "I shall never forget the frozen horror which came over us as we stood with our hands over our throats watching that terrible sight, knowing that there was no help." She later served on a state commission to investigate the Triangle fire and improve safety laws. Her work caught the attention of New York Governor Alfred Smith, who appointed

time, the group was housed and fed in an army camp and the president met with BEF leaders. Eleanor Roosevelt, the president's wife, known for her compassionate interest and active involvement in New Deal programs, visited the muddy camp to speak with the veterans about their concerns. Most of the men were offered places in the Civilian Conservation Corps, with the president waiving the age requirements in their cases.

her state industrial commissioner in 1919. When Franklin Roosevelt became governor, he kept Perkins in that position, where she supported a minimum wage law, a forty-eight-hour workweek, and laws to protect women workers.

Despite opposition, Franklin Delano Roosevelt, as president, asked Perkins to head the Labor Department. Frances Perkins decided to accept the post. Not only did she hope to improve the lot of workers and achieve other important goals; Perkins also felt a duty toward other women. As she wrote to her friend feminist Carrie Chapman Catt, "... the door might not be opened to a woman again for a long, long time and ... I had a kind of duty to other women to walk in and sit down on the chair that was offered, and so establish the right of others ... to sit in the high seats."[19]

As secretary of labor, Perkins fought to end child labor and to pass the Social Security Act of 1935, the Fair Labor Standards Act of 1938, and codes for minimum wages and a maximum number of hours for workers. Her courageous stands and hard work earned her respect from organized labor. In 1945, Perkins resigned from her Cabinet post but served on the Civil Service Commission under President Harry S. Truman. She taught at the Cornell University School of Industrial and Labor Relations from 1957 until her death in 1965.

## HELP FOR HOMEOWNERS

In June 1933, relief for homeowners arrived in the form of loans for those threatened with eviction, administered by the Home Owner's Loan Corporation (HOLC). Homeowners who could not pay their mortgages could apply for funds to refinance and arrange a plan for future payments with the HOLC. Millions of homeowners kept their dwellings with the help of the HOLC, although wages remained low and jobs were still hard to find.

## New Laws for Businesses

The National Industrial Recovery Act set up the National Recovery Administration (NRA) with initial funding of $3.3 billion. Its goal was to establish new standards for fair competition among businesses. The government said that codes should set minimum wages and maximum hours, provide for better working conditions, and abolish child labor.

Compliance was voluntary, but the administration and the public pressured leaders of business and industry to comply. These leaders were told to hold discussions until they could agree on the codes for their industries. Among the groups that developed codes were the coal, lumber, steel, garment, electric, oil, shipbuilding, and textile industries. Members of the cotton textile industry agreed to end child labor, to the joy of reformers.

Businesses that complied with NRA standards were allowed to display the NRA emblem on their windows and delivery trucks and in their advertising. The seal featured a blue eagle with the slogan "We Do Our Part." Local businesses that did not have the blue eagle were sometimes boycotted by the public.

As Roosevelt's first term drew to a close, business and government were intertwined in new and different ways. The federal budget had a large deficit, since millions of dollars had been poured into the economy. Roosevelt planned that most of the programs would be temporary, ending when the emergency subsided. At that point, he planned to curb spending and balance the federal budget.

By the summer of 1933, Roosevelt felt reassured enough to tell the public, "We are on our way."[20]

# 7

## From Depression to War

We are at peace because the world is waiting to get another gun and get it loaded.[1]

—WILL ROGERS, 1928

By 1934, there were small signs of improvement in the economy. About 5 million people who had been unemployed in 1933 now had jobs. The national income was about 50 percent higher than it had been the year before. As he moved toward the end of his first term in office, Roosevelt was ready to try more of his ideas, or what some historians call the Second New Deal.

The mid-1930s were a time of ideas, experiments, and new federal programs as the Depression continued. Natural disasters took their toll as floods plagued parts of New England and the Midwest and droughts and dust storms blighted farms and ranches in the Midwest and Plains states. As American labor leaders and workers expressed their rising discontent, there was unrest in many parts of the country. Various individuals, some with large followings, said that democracy was no longer the answer for America and suggested radical alternatives. By the end of the decade, aggressive leaders in Japan, Germany, and Italy would have mounted attacks on other countries, inciting another world war.

## Opposing the New Deal

Not everyone agreed with Roosevelt's approach, and after 1933, more-conservative Democrats and a number of Republicans opposed various programs. Some labeled his policies as socialist or even communist. The economy seemed to improve, then stall again; prosperity clearly was not around the corner.

By 1934, more lawmakers and others were vocally opposing the New Deal, prompting Roosevelt himself to admit that "the honeymoon days are over."[2] Now, the administration had to fight to get its programs through Congress.

The National Recovery Administration (NRA) came in for special criticism, since most businessmen wanted it to be abolished. They especially disliked Section 7a of the NRA rules, which gave workers the right to organize into unions and engage in collective bargaining. Yet under the NRA, employers who refused to deal with unions were not subjected to any legal penalties.

As strikes led to bloody confrontations, workers urged the administration to make even tougher laws against employers and to speak out more forcefully on their behalf. For their part, many employers blamed Roosevelt for the strife. They filed a lawsuit alleging that the NRA violated the U.S. Constitution.

On May 27, 1935, the U.S. Supreme Court agreed with them, ruling that the NRA was not constitutional. It declared that the government could *not* determine wages, working hours and conditions, or other matters of this sort unless the matters involved interstate commerce. These were legislative matters, said the Court, not under the control of the executive branch (presidency).[3] The Supreme Court was also asked to examine other New Deal programs that business leaders and others disliked. Roosevelt began to view the Court as an adversary with outmoded ideas that could impede progress and recovery from the Depression.

## FROM CRADLE TO GRAVE

One of the most famous and long-lasting pieces of legislation passed during the Roosevelt years was the Social Security Act of 1935. Poverty had brought despair to many senior citizens long before the Depression, but those years brought the problem into sharp focus. There was a consensus that something must be done. Before the act, there was no comprehensive system of pensions for the elderly, only plans here and there sponsored by certain companies, unions, or some state governments.

When Roosevelt asked Congress to approve his social security legislation, it had widespread support from both Democrats and Republicans. However, the more liberal lawmakers said the administration's plan was too limited, while conservatives said it went too far.

The final version of the act, signed into law on August 14, provided for a federal-state system of old-age pensions and unemployment compensation funded by taxes the federal government would collect from workers and employers. States that established unemployment compensation programs received this money back for use in the programs.

The highlight of the bill was protection for the elderly, guaranteeing some minimum level of income for citizens who were too old to work. At age sixty-five, workers could collect retirement benefits based on how much they had contributed during their lifetimes.

Other social services were set up, including survivors' insurance for widows and orphans, based on federal taxes received from employers and employees. This federal program initially involved 26 million Americans, the largest program ever. Roosevelt said that Americans should have a sense of security "from the cradle to the grave," and this law would greatly increase that sense of security.[4]

## LABOR UNREST

After the NRA was declared illegal, Roosevelt and his advisers drafted the National Labor Relations Act (NLRA), or Wagner Act, which Congress passed in 1935. Named for Senator Robert Wagner, it protected the rights of workers to form unions and to bargain collectively with their employers. The aim was to give workers enough security that they would spend some money, boosting the economy.

Still, there was unrest at factories and companies throughout the nation. Workers staged large sit-down strikes at an auto plant in Flint, Michigan, in both 1936 and 1937. There were strikes among longshoremen and marine workers in San Francisco. Fall brought a large-scale dispute in the textile industry when 500,000 workers refused to work. Twenty were killed, and a presidential committee was set up to investigate grievances.

A number of strikes were led by the newly strengthened Congress of Industrial Organizations (CIO). Former miner John L. Lewis had become head of the CIO, then called The Committee of Industrial Organizations, in 1935, and was determined to build up the organization. In December 1936, the CIO helped the United Auto Workers stage a successful strike. The workers negotiated with General Motors after several weeks of walkouts and demonstrations.

The CIO hoped to make inroads at U.S. Steel, long opposed to unions. With many orders for armament steel, the company was not inclined to risk strikes that would disrupt deliveries. However, smaller steel companies, such as Bethlehem Steel and National Steel, refused to negotiate with the CIO. When workers staged their walkouts in these plants, they were treated harshly. On Memorial Day 1937, a group of strikers meeting in a field in South Chicago near the Republic Steel Mill were attacked by police and factory guards. The strikers dispersed as tear gas and high-pressure water from fire hoses were aimed at them. As they were running away, about one hundred workers were shot, ten of whom died of their wounds.

A courageous group of African-American workers fought to better conditions in their profession and for all black workers. Under the leadership of A. Philip Randolph, the Brotherhood of Sleeping Car Porters pressed for better wages and working conditions for themselves and for desegregation in a variety of federal jobs. Black-run newspapers carried stories about their efforts, and porters, who traveled all over the country, distributed the newspapers so that people would be informed.

E. D. Nixon was active in the Brotherhood and later served as president of the National Association for the Advancement of Colored People (NAACP) in Montgomery, Alabama, during the peak of the Civil Rights Movement. He recalls, "When I heard Randolph speak, it was like a light. Most eloquent man I ever heard. He done more to bring me in the fight for civil rights than anybody. . . . From that day on, I was determined that I was gonna fight for freedom until I was able to get some of it myself."[5]

## A New Deal for Minorities?

The vast majority of black Americans supported Roosevelt and the New Deal policies, for the same reasons other people did. Yet the policies did not single them out for any special help and were sometimes administered in discriminatory ways, depending on where people lived.

Under some NRA codes, black citizens could be paid at lower rates than whites, and some joked that the letters NRA stood for "Negroes Ruined Again." African-American men were segregated in the CCC and TVA projects. Since the Social Security Act of 1935 excluded domestic workers and agricultural

Overall, black Americans suffered more than whites during the Depression. Roosevelt's New Deal brought some relief, since all federal relief and work programs were intended to help people in need, regardless of color. Despite the grim conditions, the Depression marked a turning point that eventually led to better times for African Americans. The growing labor movement began to enlist black members, realizing that all workers must stand together against poverty and bad working conditions. CIO unions were opened to people of color, an important development at a time when unions for steel, auto, mining, and other industries were being formed. These industries had large numbers of black employees.

Other hopeful signs: During the 1930s, the life expectancy of African Americans rose an average of five to six years. Literacy rates also rose, from 84.4 percent in 1930 to 88.5 in 1940.[6]

Changes in attitude had also occurred. Now more Americans realized what it was like to be poor and unemployed, the hopelessness and frustration that can ensue. Historians have said that the Civil Rights Movement of the 1950s and 1960s had its roots in the Great Depression.

workers, it left a great many blacks and others without protection.

Yet there was progress. Secretary of the Interior Harold Ickes assigned black executives to important posts in his department. More black professionals were employed by New Deal agencies than ever before. The Public Works Administration devoted a large share of housing to African-American citizens and built integrated housing in some communities. About 31 percent of the total wages paid out from PWA construction projects were paid to black workers.[7]

In 1937, Roosevelt appointed William Hastie, an attorney for the NAACP, as the first African-American federal judge. Two of Roosevelt's consultants, Robert Weaver and Clark Foreman, advised him on the conditions and needs of African Americans. In 1941, as more war plants were being set up, Roosevelt passed Executive Order 8802, which established the Fair Employment Practices Commission to handle complaints about discrimination toward black workers in the defense industry. But the president disappointed many Americans by not going farther in supporting civil rights legislation.

First Lady Eleanor Roosevelt worked throughout her life for the cause of racial equality. She publicly supported several laws to end discrimination against minorities. In 1939, after world-famous opera singer Marian Anderson was denied the chance to perform in Constitution Hall by the Daughters of the American Revolution (DAR), Eleanor Roosevelt resigned from the organization in protest. The First Lady arranged for Anderson to sing at the Lincoln Memorial. On that memorable night, Anderson thrilled spectators with her moving performance. The concert, with its integrated audience of more than 75,000 Americans, was a harbinger of changes to come.

## A SECOND TERM

In 1936, as Roosevelt was nominated for a second term as president, daily life had improved for many people, with fewer citizens homeless. Bank failures were part of the past, and Americans no longer feared the nation was on the brink of economic collapse. During the campaign, Roosevelt pointed out that new regulations made banks safe and prevented the excesses in the stock market that had led to the Crash. Unemployment, though still high with 9 million out of work, had gone down from the 14 million figure in 1932. And jobs were increasing as factories resumed production.

More farmers were back in business. Through flood control and conservation programs designed by the Roosevelt administration, some problems in the Dust Bowl and flood areas had been alleviated.

Republican Alf Landon, governor of Kansas, opposed Roosevelt in the 1936 presidential election. Many of Roosevelt's opponents were determined, and they had money to fight his reelection. Rumors were spread that FDR was mentally and physically unfit for office. But the New Deal triumphed as FDR won with a popular vote of 27,747,636 to 16,679,583. Only two states—Maine and Vermont—went to Landon, who received just 8 electoral votes to Roosevelt's 523. The vast majority of Americans had endorsed Roosevelt's programs, and thousands withstood the rain on January 20, 1937, to see FDR's second inauguration. The Twentieth Amendment to the Constitution (called the "Lame Duck" Amendment) had moved the inauguration date up from March to January. Americans had been frustrated in 1933 by the months of waiting before FDR could be sworn in and set his programs in motion. The charismatic leader spoke forcefully about the need to push forward, to fight against the lingering economic problems that faced the nation.

As he began his new term, Roosevelt was increasingly concerned that the U.S. Supreme Court would destroy his programs. In 1937, he suggested that Congress pass legislation increasing the number of justices from nine to fifteen and requiring them to retire at age sixty-five. This proposal, which opponents called "packing the Court," was defeated. Eventually, Roosevelt would be able to appoint four new justices to replace those on the Court who died or retired.

The New Deal received a boost in 1937 when the Court ruled that both the Social Security and Wagner Acts were constitutional. In its ruling on the Wagner Act, the Court said that workers had a fundamental right to organize and that such a right was needed if they were "to deal on an equality with their employer."[8] Nor did the Court strike down the Second Agricultural Adjustment Act, passed to aid farmers in 1938.

## CRISES ABROAD

As Americans continued to grapple with the Depression, people in other nations faced fascism and imperialism. Just as Americans had turned to new political ideas and new leaders to deal with their economic crises, so had the citizens of other countries.

In Germany, where people faced widespread economic problems and loss of national pride that had resulted from World War I, Adolf Hitler was elected. His new political party, called the National Socialists, known as Nazis, established a military state in Germany. There was censorship and persecution of Jews and other minorities, whom Hitler scapegoated as the "cause" of Germany's problems. In 1936, Nazi troops defied the Treaty of Versailles, which had ended World War I, and marched into the demilitarized zone called the Rhineland.

Mussolini's fascist government maintained a firm hold in Italy, invading Ethiopia in 1935, while in Spain, General Francisco Franco moved to upset the democratic government. It became ever more clear that Hitler and Mussolini fully intended to take over other nations, perhaps even all of Europe. In addition, powerful military leaders in Japan were invading China and seemed bent on taking over all its territory.

Although during the dark days of the thirties, Americans had heard from many individuals who wanted to overthrow democracy, no revolution had taken place. Roosevelt spoke about this in his fireside chat of April 14, 1938:

> History proves that dictatorships do not grow out of strong and successful governments, but out of weak and helpless ones. If by democratic methods people get a government strong enough to

protect them from fear and starvation, their democracy succeeds; but if they do not, they grow impatient. Therefore, the only sure bulwark of continuing liberty is a government strong enough to protect the interests of the people, and a people strong enough and well enough informed to maintain its sovereign control over its government. We are a rich Nation; we can afford to pay for security and prosperity without having to sacrifice our liberties in the bargain.[9]

Still mired in the Depression, most Americans were not pre-occupied with foreign affairs. As news of Nazi persecution of Jews reached the United States, many people condemned Hitler but

---

### ∼ *RADICAL IDEAS* ∼

As people grew impatient for an end to the Depression, some turned to new and radical ideas. On the left, socialist and com-munist candidates won more support in congressional and state elections. Roosevelt was urged to go farther to the left in his policies and programs.

A number of vocal people in the United States espoused extreme political solutions to the nation's woes. Some were anarchists who said that Americans should overthrow the gov-ernment and establish a noncapitalistic system.

Right-leaning fascists claimed large groups of followers. A follower of Hitler, William Dudley Pelley, led a group called the Silver Shirts. They hoped to overthrow the government and get rid of Jews, Catholics, people of color, and others Pelley viewed as "undesirable."

The outspoken and controversial Governor Huey Long of Louisiana, who exercised great control over politics in his state, believed that wealth should be redistributed in the nation. Under Long's "Share Our Wealth" movement, each person would receive at least $5,000 a year when the wealthiest

---

did not support active U.S. involvement in Germany's political affairs. The invasion of Ethiopia and unprovoked Japanese attacks on China likewise drew criticism from Americans. But most citizens and many politicians favored a neutral policy of staying out of European wars in the future.

Roosevelt opposed a neutral stance. In 1937, he called for an international quarantine against aggressor nations, and a slight majority of Americans agreed. There was no support for military retaliation against Japan, though, after they bombed and sank an American gunboat, the *Panay*, in December 1937. The Japanese were told that an apology and payment for damages would suffice.

citizens—those with more than $5 million—were forced to give up their holdings. More than 4.6 million people agreed with Long's program and his plan to charge a 100 percent tax on incomes of more than $1 million a year. The money would be used to buy every American family a "homestead"—a house, car, and other necessities—and give everyone a minimum annual family income of $2,000 to $3,000, plus old-age pensions, educational benefits, and veterans' pensions. A former follower shot and killed Long in 1935.

In 1934, Father Charles Coughlin, a Catholic priest broadcasting a radio program out of Chicago, received more mail than any other American.[10] Coughlin had been on the radio since 1929, calling for a redistribution of wealth and criticizing Wall Street, bankers, and various government policies. He initially supported the New Deal, but by the late thirties was calling for an end to capitalism in the United States. He supported policies of some fascist leaders in Europe, expressing anti-Semitic (anti-Jewish) attitudes. After he began praising Adolf Hitler, the leaders of the Roman Catholic Church ordered the "Radio Priest" to stop his program.

## A Boost for Defense Industries

In March 1938, Hitler's troops marched into and annexed Austria. Apprehensive, the leaders of England and France placed orders with U.S. companies for planes, tanks, guns, and other weapons. These nations also began to store food, much of it ordered from the United States, in anticipation of war.

Early in 1939, Roosevelt asked Congress to approve $300 million in defense spending, warning that foreign powers threatened U.S. security and the nation should build up its own military arsenal. Within weeks after Roosevelt made this speech, in mid-March Hitler led his troops into Czechoslovakia; Mussolini, now allied with Hitler, invaded Albania.

As orders came in, U.S. industries stepped up production and hired more employees. A total of 6 million people, half of them minorities, remained out of work, but now people hoped that America had not only turned the corner but was on the road to prosperity again.

With turmoil abroad, Americans voted Franklin Roosevelt into an unprecedented third term as president. They chose the man who had navigated the country through the Depression to lead the United States through what would be the most destructive war in history.

War became certain in 1940 when Germany invaded Poland. At once, Poland's allies, England and France, declared war on Germany. Although not at war itself, the United States supplied the Allied nations with more arms and raw materials.

## At War!

Early on the morning of December 7, 1941, Japanese planes attacked the U.S. naval base at Pearl Harbor, in Hawaii. With that, Congress declared war on Japan, prompting her Axis allies to declare war on the United States. Young Americans who had come of age during the Great Depression now faced a war.

As men enlisted or were drafted into the service and more jobs opened up in war plants, the Great Depression was finally ending. There had been 8 million unemployed Americans in 1939; that figure dropped to 4 million in 1940. By 1941, there was virtually no unemployment, since everyone who sought a job could find one. The fact that people were so eager to work when there *was* work disproved the critics who had said that public welfare programs sponsored by the New Deal would create a lazy population who preferred government handouts over self-sufficiency.

No longer confronting the uncertainty and hardships of the Depression, Americans now faced new perils and sacrifices. The generation that had survived the Depression now had to get through four years of war.

# 8

~

# The Legacy of the Depression

World ain't going to be saved by nobody's scheme. It's fellows with schemes that got us into this mess. Plans get you into things but you got to work your way out.[1]

—WILL ROGERS, 1931

The Great Depression brought suffering, lost dreams, death, and devastation. It also strengthened individuals and families, inspired great works of literature and art, and brought strong political leaders to the fore. During the thirties, Americans had to reexamine their ideas about economics and politics and rethink how American capitalism should operate.

Despite all their efforts, Roosevelt and his Brain Trust had not found a cure for all the nation's economic woes. Rather, historians would say that Roosevelt's greatest contribution was in restoring hope and confidence to the American people and giving enough direct relief to enable individuals to survive.

Roosevelt had tried to deal with emergency conditions in innovative, experimental ways. As author John Rublowsky would say, "There was no ideological basis behind these programs but rather a philosophical sympathy towards the suffering caused by the depression."[2] The president had used his energy and personal appeal to build up confidence in America and its ability to rebound from catastrophe. Many historians thus think the most powerful effects of the New Deal were "more psychological than economic."

Rublowsky and others believe that "The New Deal, though it did much to alleviate some of the more desperate effects of the collapse, was not bringing recovery."[3] Yet, the New Deal kept the American system of democracy functioning during a time when democratic governments collapsed around the world.

Goldston says there was a central question involved:

> Can a society based on free enterprise—whose citizens are raised from the cradle to believe in competition as the basis of life, and the success of the individual (no matter what the private or public cost) in that competition as the ultimate good—provide a just, inspiring, secure, or even sane framework for the human body, mind, and spirit? And if not, what kind of society could possibly take its place? Certainly not a regimented one, or one in which the worship of success is replaced by the worship of the state (or of any state dogma, philosophy, or public religion). One of the great accomplishments of the New Deal was to keep the future open to answer this question. . . . Neither Fascism or Communism nor any variants thereon were substituted for honest and energetic experimentation, questioning, and exploration. So long as the future *remains* open there is reason to hope that problems— slowly, painfully perhaps, but progressively—*can* be solved.[4]

In 1945, shortly after being elected to his fourth term, Roosevelt died. Former New Dealer David Morse was now in the Army. He recalled, "I sat down on the curbside and cried. That was the end of a period, the end of a chapter. But by then we were in our thirties."[5]

## END OF THE PROGRAMS

As the wartime economy brought jobs and renewed prosperity, some New Deal programs changed while others were terminated.

In 1942, the CCC, a favorite of ardent conservationist Roosevelt, ended. The Corps had built 46,854 bridges; 3,116 fire-lookout towers; more than 28 million rods of fencing; 318,076 check dams for erosion control; and 33,087 miles of terracing. It had planted millions of trees and acres of grass, and excavated channels, canals, and ditches. Around the nation, it had improved wildlife habitat and built or maintained thousands of miles of hiking trails, what former corpsman Donald Dale Jackson called, ". . . a splendid heritage of parks, dams, bridges, buildings, roads, and hundreds of conservation and restoration projects in every corner of the country."[6] Forty-seven corpsmen had been killed while fighting forest fires. Another 300 had died when a hurricane in the Florida Keys streaked through three CCC camps there.

Other former corpsmen have reflected on their work. Says Harry Dallas of Missouri, "We built something and I knew I helped and I saw the result. It was something you could take pride in, and there wasn't a lot of pride in those days."[7] Arthur Jackson adds, "I'm proud that I worked on that Crossville [Tennessee] dam. I wasn't afraid to tackle anything after that."[8]

Says Robert Ritchie, from Hansell, Iowa, who worked at Backbone Park: "As you go on, you feel that it, that you, were a part of the country and of history. We have this park; it was wilderness before, and now it's a nice place to go, and I had something to do with that."[9]

## GOVERNMENT INVOLVEMENT IN OUR LIVES

Since the thirties, the federal government has played a larger role in many areas of American life where it had been less involved before—relief for those in need, agriculture, the stock exchange, and labor relations, to name a few. A number of new buildings went up in Washington, D.C., as the federal government increased its areas of responsibility. It became involved in agriculture, business, distributing pensions to older Americans, lending money, and increased its control of interstate commerce. The number of government employees rose from 580,000 in 1931 to more than 1,370,000 in 1941.

These numbers continued to grow after the forties, with more regulatory agencies and programs and ever higher federal budgets. People disagree on whether these changes are for the better or not. During different election years, candidates have debated what kind of, and how much, government the American people need.

The New Deal marked a change in outlook about the duty a government has for its citizens. With the passage of the Social Security Act of 1935, the government was stating that it believed it had social responsibility for the welfare of its citizens. However, a number of Americans opposed Social Security and other government-run social programs. Historians often point out that Roosevelt himself saw most of his social programs, Social Security being a major exception, as temporary measures to ease an unusual crisis. In fact, while the New Deal was being developed, some of Roosevelt's advisers told him that giving people money outright, such as through sending them checks in the mail, would be cheaper than running the CCC, WPA, and other work programs. Roosevelt and a number of his supporters opposed programs not linked directly to work. The president worried that such "giveaways" might destroy the American work ethic and harm the nation in the long run. He might well have expressed surprise and concern about some of the welfare programs that developed in the United States after the 1940s.

## A WAR ON POVERTY

The end of the Depression and World War II left unfinished business in America. Equality for African Americans, Latinos, and other minorities was a dream yet to be realized. Black Americans, with the support of many whites, led the way in the Civil Rights Movement of the 1950s and 1960s, which encouraged women, Native Americans, and others to fight for their rights to equal opportunities in housing, jobs, education, and other areas of life. Many historians believe that these movements were born in the Depression, a time when citizens began to see they had more power to influence the government.

During the 1960s, more Americans became aware that although the nation as a whole was prosperous, there were millions living in poverty in the richest land on earth. Rural farmers, people in Appalachia, migrant workers, and others often worked and lived in terrible conditions. It was clear that in many cases, poor citizens had suffered from discrimination and other factors that kept families in poverty for generations.

A number of the nation's political leaders had come of age during the Depression. After becoming president in 1963, former New Dealer Lyndon B. Johnson announced that his administration would wage a "war on poverty." Johnson was familiar with the plight of the poor. He had risen from humble roots himself and later taught children of migrant workers and poor immigrants in Texas. He had served with the National Youth Administration during the Depression years.

Shortly after taking office, Johnson urged the passage of new and more comprehensive civil rights legislation. In his State of the Union message, he said,

> Unfortunately many Americans live on the outskirts of hope— some because of their poverty, and some because of their color, and all too many because of both. Our task is to help replace their despair with opportunity. . . . This administration today here and now declares unconditional war on poverty in America.[10]

During 1965, Johnson's Great Society legislation included the Medicare Act, which provided medical, hospital, and nursing care coverage for elderly Americans, and the Medicaid program, which provided government health insurance to people living in poverty. Education and employment were priorities in the war on poverty. A popular program called Operation Head Start initially enrolled 750,000 pre-school-age children in schools linked with other social services, such as health care. The program continues today and has been praised for helping to prepare disadvantaged children for school. Johnson's aid-to-education laws distributed $1 billion to school districts serving poor children, and more loans were made available to help the poor pursue higher education. New job training programs under the Economic Opportunity Act of 1964 tried to break the cycle of poverty.

Surveys had shown that 10 million Americans were suffering from hunger, and the Johnson administration expanded school lunch programs and developed a program to provide money for women and children's nutrition programs.

These programs expanded the role of the federal government and took more control away from the individual states. As had been the case during previous years, politicians, citizens, and others challenged the Great Society programs and complained about government "handouts." During the 1980s, more and more citizens and legislators challenged the idea of social welfare programs. Throughout the eighties and nineties, people proposed new ways to end or curtail welfare programs and to make sure that they reached only people who were too sick, old, or disabled to work.

Do social programs "work"? Since the 1930s, this has been debated continually in America. In 1993, federal, state, and local governments spent about $300 billion on programs to aid the poor.[11] This included the following programs: Medicaid $132 billion, food stamps $26 billion, Supplemental Security Income (SSI) $26 billion, Aid to Families with Dependent Children $25 billion, low-income housing subsidies $20 billion, Head Start and other compensatory education programs $10 billion.

SSI was created in 1972 during the Nixon presidency to give cash benefits to the poor and provides a minimum monthly income to the disabled and the elderly. Congress also increased Social Security benefits for these people in 1972. After that year, poverty among the elderly decreased from 19 percent to 15 percent in 1982, to 12 percent in 1992.

Social Security has remained one of the most popular of the New Deal social welfare programs, and few legislators have suggested ending it, although some political leaders have proposed changes in the current system. Proposals to reduce or delay benefits or impose higher taxes on those receiving Social Security have met with strong resistance from powerful lobbying groups made up of elderly citizens.

After several years of debate, Congress did pass a major welfare reform law in 1996. The new welfare law gives more control over social welfare programs to individual states. Among other things, the law limits the number of years able-bodied people may collect welfare benefits. It states that adults on welfare who can work should perform community service jobs in exchange for benefits if other jobs are not available in the private or public sector.

President Clinton and other political leaders expressed the hope that these approaches, coupled with health care reform and education and job-training programs, will improve the current system and prevent families from becoming caught in the "welfare cycle." Finding effective ways to address the problems of poverty in America, which have always existed to some degree, remains a challenge.

## ANOTHER DEPRESSION?

From time to time, people have pointed to certain conditions in the economy and warned that another massive depression might arise. There have been ups and downs in the economy since the Great Depression, with recessions occurring through the years.

Many Americans feared that depression would follow World War II, as had happened after World War I. Instead, the economy grew rapidly for two decades after the war. During the last half of the twentieth century, there were fluctuations in the economy and times of recession but nothing approaching the magnitude of the Great Depression. There have also been slumps in specific industries.

But the American free enterprise system is different than it was in 1929. Labor unions, although their membership makes up a much smaller percentage of the total workforce than it once did, are strong and active, and the idea of a forty-hour workweek, set by the defunct NRA, persisted after the thirties.

Even though the NRA was ruled unconstitutional in 1935, changes had already taken place, and the National Labor Relations Act cemented the rights of workers and organized labor even more. It banned management from interfering with the organization of unions or other collective-bargaining activities and required management to deal with those representatives chosen by the employees. It made it illegal to "blacklist" people from jobs because of their involvement in unions. Unions became broader in scope, including members of different trades and professions. The CIO included mine workers, garment workers, and those in the oil, gas, and refinery industries, among others. Robert Goldston says, "The strength of American labor unions assures that increases in productivity are matched (and now sometimes overmatched) by increases in pay and purchasing power."[12]

Strong labor organizations have been able to influence policies in new, powerful ways. They gained strong financial support as large numbers of people became involved in their efforts. Unions formed strong political blocs as well, as they became involved in selecting, contributing campaign money to, and voting for the candidates of their choice.

The distribution of wealth has changed in America although there are still enormous gaps between rich and poor. No longer is 40 percent of the nation's wealth held by only 5 percent of all Americans. Today's economy is not as dependent upon the buying of luxury items. The companies that depended on those kinds of sales failed quickly after the Depression began, while industries that provided services people must have to live fared better.

Roosevelt had wanted a change in the distribution of wealth. According to Milton Katz, a lawyer who worked under both Hoover and Roosevelt, "Under Franklin Roosevelt, democratic liberalism, coming into power in the Great Depression, was fully alive to the paramount importance of economic growth, productivity, and employment. Committed also to the welfare of the ill-fed, ill-clothed, and ill-housed, it undertook to develop economic growth and social equity as mutually supporting objectives. FDR said, 'Above all else, I want to restore balance to American life. We have totally neglected the people who fell behind in the process of developing America.' "[13]

The stock market is subject to far more control and more regulations today than ever before. The Securities and Exchange Commission (SEC) can limit margin buying, can moderate extreme fluctuations of prices in the market, and can prosecute people who try to manipulate stock prices or mislead or cheat consumers. It strictly regulates the way that new stock offerings can be presented to customers. The Federal Reserve Board has control over interest rates, and the SEC can require people to pay higher rates for buying stock on margin, or even insist on full payment. The amount of margin debt investors can accumulate is limited by the cash value of their brokerage account, another way of preventing overspeculation.

No longer are there huge investment trusts as there were before the Crash. The kinds of investment funds that exist now are carefully regulated and monitored. Commercial banks may not use deposits to speculate in the stock market, and bank deposits are insured by the federal government, which would prevent the massive loss of savings that occurred in 1929. The Federal Reserve Board regulates U.S. banking practices. Banks must use the interest rate established by this government agency in establishing the rates at which they lend money to customers. In an emergency, banks could borrow money from the "Fed."

Bankruptcy laws were changed. The Banking Act of 1933 and other new laws set forth the process of reorganization and legal steps that would be taken if companies got into trouble.

But speculation still happens, and stock prices sometimes seem to rise above the actual value of a company. Historian Robert Goldston says, "The glittering dream of something for nothing dies hard in the human breast; it will, no doubt, one day manifest itself again and, inevitably, lead to stock collapse."[14]

## LESSONS FROM THOSE WHO LIVED IT

Living through the Depression, with its fears and uncertainties, had a profound effect on the values cherished by many Americans and on the way they lived their lives afterward. Iola Voltman of Baldwin, Wisconsin, says, "When the Great Depression survivors went out into the world and found work with meager pay, they were willing to forgo all the little things, saving frugally for years, for the big things they were afraid they'd never acquire. There was no easy way to get a foothold, or to get a start at anything."[15]

Gordon Parks arrived in Washington, D.C., in 1939 as a photographer for the Farm Security Administration. One of his first tasks was to study the photos that had been taken by the great photographers of the thirties—Dorothea Lange, Russell Lee, Ben Shahn, Jack Delano, and others. He later wrote about his feelings as he studied these images of "the gutted cotton fields, the eroded farmland, the crumbling South, the unending lines of dispossessed migrants, the pitiful shacks, the shameful city ghettos, the breadlines and bonus marchers, the gaunt faces of men, women, and children caught up in the tragedy; the horrifying spectacles of sky blackened with locusts, and swirling dust and towns flooded with muddy rivers. . . ."[16] The photographs were poignant reminders of human suffering.

Says B. Sampson of Fort Dodge, Iowa, "The Depression taught us thrift and conservation. I tried to pass this concept on to my children, and I think some was retained, but I don't see any hope for my grandchildren in this instant-gratification, throwaway society."[17]

Sandra Harson of Knoxville, Iowa, recalls that while growing up in the early 1940s, she and her family

> . . . never felt as though we were poor. Dad had a knack for making fun from even the most disagreeable tasks with his endless stories, poems, and riddles. And even when there was little to put on the table, Mom could stretch what we had and make it look lovely to look at, besides. . . . The deprivation my parents had endured just a few years before I was born made them realize the importance of instilling in their own children the joy of small pleasures and the priceless treasure of love in a family.[18]

Many who lived through the Depression learned to appreciate simpler pleasures and fewer material things, and some continued to worry throughout their lives about economic security. Many found themselves unable to waste anything, especially food.

Theirs was a generation that went from economic catastrophe to a devastating world war, and many said they were able to survive that second challenge because they had been toughened by the first. For a while, the money had stopped, and human want and need had reached epidemic proportions. But the nation and its people had endured.

# Source Notes

### CHAPTER 1

1. Donald Day, ed., *The Autobiography of Will Rogers* (New York: Lancer, 1932), 171.

2. Dixon Wecter, *The Age of the Great Depression: 1929–41* (New York: Macmillan, 1948), 1.

3. Robert Goldston, *The Great Depression: The United States in the Thirties* (New York: Fawcett Premium Books, 1968), 37.

4. Ibid., 22.

5. Herbert Hoover, *The Memoirs of Herbert Hoover* (New York: Macmillan, 1952), vol. 3, 27.

6. Ibid., 21.

7. Goldston, 33.

8. John Kenneth Galbraith, "Why the Money Stopped," in *A Sense of History: The Best Writing from the Pages of American Heritage* (New York: American Heritage Press, 1985), 671.

9. Caroline Bird, *The Invisible Scar: The Great Depression and What It Did to American Life, From Then Until Now* (New York: David McKay, 1966), 7.

10. T. H. Watkins, *The Great Depression: America in the 1930s* (Boston: Little, Brown, 1993), 69.

11. Day, 160.

12. Bryan Sterling, ed., *The Best of Will Rogers* (New York: Crown, 1979), n.p.

13. Quoted in Richard N. Current, John A. Garrity, and Julius

Weinberg, eds., *Words That Made American History Since the Civil War* (Boston: Little, Brown, 1972), 380.

14. John A. Garraty, *The Great Depression: An Inquiry into the Causes, Course, and Consequence of the Worldwide Depression of the Nineteen-Thirties, as Seen by Contemporaries and in the Light of History* (New York: Harcourt Brace Jovanovich, 1986), 645.

15. Day, 190.


### CHAPTER 2

1. Day, *Autobiography of Will Rogers*, 232.

2. Bird, *The Invisible Scar*, 7.

3. Goldston, *The Great Depression*, 40.

4. Gordon Parks, *A Choice of Weapons* (New York: Harper & Row, 1966), 55.

5. Isabel Lee, "The Depression is Why She's a Democrat," *Westport (CT) Minuteman* (October 5, 1995), 20.

6. Richard Lowitt and Maurine Beasley, eds., *One Third of a Nation: Lorena Hickok Reports on the Great Depression* (Urbana: University of Illinois Press, 1981), xi.

7. Ibid., 159.

8. Moses Crutchfield, "Class of '37 Endured Tough Times," *Greensboro (NC) News and Record* (February 1987), op-ed.

9. Day, 212.


### CHAPTER 3

1. Sterling, *The Best of Will Rogers*, 95.

2. Bird, *The Invisible Scar*, 53.

3. From the Eleanor Roosevelt papers, quoted in Robert S. McElvaine, *Down and Out in the Great Depression: Letters from the "Forgotten Man"* (Chapel Hill: University of North Carolina Press, 1983), 172.

4. Ibid.

5. Penny Colman, *Rosie the Riveter* (New York: Crown, 1994), 24–25.

6. Adrian Paradis, *The Hungry Years* (Philadelphia: Chilton, 1967) 42–46.

7. Goldston, *The Great Depression*, 49–50.

8. Edward Ellis, *A Nation in Torment: The Great Depression* (New York: Coward McCann, 1970), 243.

9. Lowitt and Beasley, *One Third of a Nation*, 365.

10. Ibid., 364.

11. Ibid.

12. Paradis, 78–80.

13. Russell Baker, *Growing Up* (New York: St. Martin's Press, 1982), 98.

14. Quoted in Irving Werstein, *A Nation Fights Back: The Depression and Its Aftermath* (New York: Julian Messner, 1962), 133.

15. Watkins, *The Great Depression*, 95–98.

CHAPTER 4

1. Day, *Autobiography of Will Rogers*, 230.

2. Studs Terkel, *Hard Times: An Oral History of the Great Depression* (New York: Pantheon, 1970), 7.

3. Milton Meltzer, *Brother, Can You Spare a Dime? The Great Depression 1929–1933* (New York: Alfred A. Knopf, 1969), 212.

4. Ibid., 214.

5. From *The Nation* (September 9, 1931); quoted in Meltzer, 218.

6. Milton Meltzer, *The Black Americans: A History in Their Own Words 1619–1983* (New York: Crowell, 1984), 218.

7. Parks, *A Choice of Weapons*, 156.

8. Lowitt and Beasley, *One Third of a Nation*, 186.

9. Quoted in Meltzer, *The Black Americans*, 228.

10. Bird, *The Invisible Scar*, 26.

11. Lowitt and Beasley, 26.

12. Ibid., 27.

13. Ibid., 23.

14. David J. Wilson, "Growing Up During the Depression," *Cobblestone* (March, 1984), 17.

15. Dennis Brindell Fradin, *Disaster! Drought* (Chicago: Childrens Press, 1983), 18.

16. Ibid.

17. Jerry Stanley, *Children of the Dust Bowl: The True Story of the School at Weedpatch Camp* (New York: Crown, 1992), 11.

18. Quoted in Richard O'Connor, *John Steinbeck* (New York: McGraw Hill, 1970), 63.

19. Quoted in Stanley, 1.

20. Stanley, 37.

21. Terkel, 53.

## CHAPTER 5

1. Sterling, *The Best of Will Rogers*, 96.

2. Cabell Phillips, *From the Crash to the Blitz: 1929–1939* (New York: Macmillan, 1969), 34.

3. Susan Ware, *Holding Their Own: American Women in the 1930s* (Boston: Twayne Publishers, 1982), 5.

4. Interview with the author.

5. Donald Dale Jackson, "They Were Poor, Hungry, and They Built to Last," *Smithsonian* (December 1994), 69.

6. Rita Van Amber, *Stories and Recipes of the Great Depression of the 1930s, vol. 2* (Menomonie, Wis.: Van Amber Publishers, 1993), 48.

7. Letter to the author.

8. Letter; interview with the author.

9. Interview with the author.

10. Ibid.

11. Bird, *The Invisible Scar*, 100.

12. Ibid., 101.

13. Ware, 73.

14. Baker, *Growing Up*, 115–116.

15. Ibid., 117.

16. Ibid., 144.

17. Peter Irons, *The Courage of Their Convictions* (New York: The Free Press, 1988), 25–26.

18. Ibid.

19. Fred Von Gunten, "Depression Gifts of the Magi," *Prevention's 20th Anniversary Edition* (Christmas, 1994), 6.

20. Van Amber, 73.

21. Goldston, *The Great Depression*, 100.

### CHAPTER 6

1. Day, *Autobiography of Will Rogers*, 278.

2. Werstein, *A Nation Fights Back*, 140.

3. Quoted in Current, Garrity, and Weinberg, *Words That Made American History*, 380, 405.

4. Ibid.

5. Ibid., 406.

6. Goldston, *The Great Depression*, 91.

7. Current et al., 408.

8. Ibid., 409.

9. Phillips, *From the Crash to the Blitz*, 264.

10. Current et al., 395.

11. Katie Louchheim, ed., *The Making of the New Deal: Insiders Speak* (Cambridge, Mass.: Harvard University Press, 1983), xvi.

12. Ibid., 16.

13. Jackson, "They Were Poor, Hungry, and They Built to Last," 68.

14. Ibid., 66.

15. Ibid., 75.

16. Jordan A. Schwartz, *The New Dealers: Power Politics in the Age of Roosevelt* (New York: Alfred A. Knopf, 1993), 202.

17. McElvaine, *Down and Out in the Great Depression*, 153.

18. Phillips, 271.

19. Ware, *Holding Their Own*, 92.

20. John Rublowsky, *After the Crash: America in the Great Depression* (Crowell-Collier, 1970), 131.

### Chapter 7

1. Day, *Autobiography of Will Rogers*, 177.

2. Werstein, *A Nation Fights Back*, 156.

3. Watkins, *The Great Depression*, 240–41.

4. Bird, *The Invisible Scar*, 205.

5. Terkel, *Hard Times*, 119.

6. Robert S. McElvaine, *The Great Depression: America 1929–1941* (New York: Times Books, 1984), 194.

7. Ibid.

8. Werstein, 163.

9. Franklin D. Roosevelt, Public Papers and Addresses (S. I. Rosenman, ed., 1938–1941, 242–243), in Arthur M. Schlesinger and Dixon Ryan Fox, eds., *A History of American Life: The Age of the Great Depression* (New York: Macmillian, 1949), n.p.

10. Ware, *Holding Their Own*, xv.

### Chapter 8

1. Day, *Autobiography of Will Rogers*, 315.

2. Rublowsky, *After the Crash*, 150.

3. Ibid., 151.

4. Goldston, *The Great Depression*, 198.

5. Louchheim, *The Making of the New Deal*, 95.

6. Jackson, "They Were Poor, Hungry, and They Built to Last," 67.

7. Ibid., 76.

8. Ibid., 78.

9. Ibid., 69.

10. Lyndon B. Johnson, State of the Union Address, January 8, 1964; in Arthur M. Schlesinger, ed., *The State of the Union*

*Messages of the Presidents 1790–1966* (New York, Chelsea House, 1966), vol. 3, 3157.

11. Susan Mayer and Christopher Jenks, "War on Poverty: No Apologies, Please," *New York Times* ( November 9, 1995), A29.

12. Goldston, 195.

13. Louchheim, 129.

14. Goldston, 194.

15. Van Amber, *Stories and Recipes of the Great Depression*, 2.

16. Parks, *A Choice of Weapons*, 228.

17. Van Amber, 2.

18. Ibid., 78.

# Further Reading

(An asterisk indicates a book written for young people.)

Adamic, Louis. *My America*. New York: Harper & Row, 1938.

*Bernstein, Irving. *A Caring Society: The New Deal, the Worker, and the Great Depression*. Boston: Houghton Mifflin, 1985.

*———. *The Lean Years*. Baltimore: Penguin, 1966.

Botkin, B. A. *Sidewalks of America*. New York: Bobbs-Merrill, 1954.

Bremer, William W. *Depression Winters: New York Social Workers and the New Deal*. Philadelphia: Temple University Press, 1984.

Brinkley, Alan. *Voices of Protest: Huey Long, Father Coughlin, and the Great Depression*. New York: Alfred A. Knopf, 1982.

Brooks, Thomas R. *Picket Lines and Bargaining Tables: Organized Labor Comes of Age, 1933–1945*. New York: Grosset & Dunlap, 1968.

Chambers, Clark A., ed. *The New Deal at Home and Abroad*. New York: Macmillan, 1965.

*Farrell, Jacqueline. *The Great Depression*. San Diego: Lucent, 1996.

Federal Writers Project. *These Are Our Lives*. Chapel Hill: University of North Carolina Press, 1939.

Feis, Herbert. *1933: Characters in Crisis*. Boston: Little, Brown, 1966.

Freidel, Frank. *Franklin D. Roosevelt: A Rendezvous With Destiny*. Boston: Little, Brown, 1990.

Galbraith, John. *The Great Crash, 1929*. Boston: Houghton Mifflin, 1955.

Garraty, John A. *The American Nation: A History of the United States Since 1865*. New York: Harper & Row, 1979.

Gipe, George. *The Great American Sports Book*. Garden City, N.Y.: Doubleday, 1978.

*Glassman, Bruce. *The Crash of '29 and the New Deal*. Morristown, N.J.: Silver Burdett, 1986.

Gregory, James. *American Exodus: The Dust Bowl Migration and Okie Culture in California*. New York: Oxford University Press, 1989.

*Hacker, Jeffrey H. *Franklin D. Roosevelt*. New York: Lothrop, Lee and Shepard, 1981.

Johnson, Charles S. *The Shadow of the Plantation*. University of Chicago Press, 1934.

*Katz, William Loren. *An Album of the Great Depression*. New York: Franklin Watts, 1978.

Kirby, John B. *Black Americans in the Roosevelt Era: Liberalism and Race*. Knoxville: University of Tennessee Press, 1980.

Lacy, Leslie Alexander. *The Soil Soldiers: The Civilian Conservation Corps in the Great Depression*. Radnor, Pa.: Chilton, 1976.

Lynd, R. S. *Middletown in Transition*. New York: Harcourt Brace Jovanovich, 1937.

Mangione, Jerre. *The Dream and the Deal: The Federal Writers Project, 1935–1943*. Philadelphia: University of Pennsylvania Press, 1983.

Martin, George. *Madame Secretary: Frances Perkins*. Boston: Houghton Mifflin, 1976.

*Meltzer, Milton. *Dorothea Lange: Life Through the Camera*. New York: Viking, 1985.

Parish, Michael E. *Anxious Decades: America in Prosperity and Depression, 1920–1941*. New York: W. W. Norton, 1992.

Perrett, Geoffrey. *Days of Sadness, Years of Triumph: The American People, 1939–1945*. Madison: University of Wisconsin Press, 1973.

Peterson, Robert Trescott. *The Great Boom and Panic: 1921–29*. Chicago: Henry Regnery, 1965.

Rogers, Agnes. *I Remember Distinctly*. New York: Harper & Bros., 1947.

Roosevelt, Eleanor. *My Day* (Her Acclaimed Columns, 1936–1945.) New York: Pharos, 1989.

Ruiz, Vicki L. *Cannery Women, Cannery Lives: Mexican Women, Unionization, and the California Food Processing Industry, 1930–1950*. Albuquerque: University of New Mexico Press, 1987.

Schlesinger, Arthur M., Jr. *The Age of Roosevelt: The Coming of the New Deal*. Boston: Houghton Mifflin, 1958.

———. *The Age of Roosevelt: The Politics of Upheaval*. Boston: Houghton Mifflin, 1959.

Shannon, David A., ed. *The Great Depression*. Englewood Cliffs, N.J.: Prentice-Hall, 1960.

Smith, Page. *Redeeming the Time: A People's History of the 1920s and New Deal*. New York: McGraw-Hill, 1987.

*Sonneborn, Liz. *Will Rogers: Cherokee Entertainer*. New York: Chelsea House, 1993.

Stein, Walter. *California and the Dust Migration*. Westport, Conn.: Greenwood Press, 1973.

Steinbeck, John. *The Grapes of Wrath*. New York: Viking, 1967.

———. *Their Blood Is Strong*. San Francisco: Simon J. Lubin Society, 1938.

*Stewart, Gail B. *The New Deal*. New York: Macmillan, 1993.

Thomas, Gordon, and Max Morgan-Witts. *The Day the Bubble Burst: A Social History of the Wall Street Crash of 1929*. Garden City, N.Y.: Doubleday, 1979.

Weiner, Lynn W. *From Working Girl to Working Mother: The Female Labor Force in the United States 1820–1980*. Chapel Hill, N.C.: University of North Carolina Press, 1985.

*Wormser, Richard. *Growing Up in the Great Depression*. New York: Atheneum, 1994.

———. *Hoboes: Wandering in America, 1870–1940*. New York: Walker, 1994.

# Index

strikes, 90–91

Supplemental Security Income (SSI), 105–106

tenant farming, 51–53

Tennessee Valley Authority (TVA), 82–83

Terkel, Studs, 48–49

textile industry, 14, 90

trading for goods and services, 64–65

Treaty of Versailles, 95

Triangle Factory fire, 84–85

Truman, Harry S., 85

Truth-in-Securities Act, 76

Twenty-first Amendment, 78–79

U.S. Food Administration, 18

unemployment, 26, 27–29, 32, 35–37, 42, 48, 49, 99

unions, 13, 58, 90, 91, 107–108

United Farmworkers Union of America, 58

Volstead Act, 78–79

Wagner Act, 90, 94–95

Wagner, Robert, 90

Wallace, Henry A., 81

Waters, Walter W., 44

welfare programs, 105, 106

Will Rogers Memorial, 19

Wilson, Woodrow, 18

women, unemployment of, 37

Woodin, William, 74

Works Progress Administration (WPA), 83

World War I, 11, 15

World War II, 95–98, 107

# About the Author

Victoria Sherrow is the author of more than forty books for young people on topics such as endangered mammals, the health care system, bioethics, and American politics. She resides in Connecticut with her husband and three children.

DATE DUE